CORE ADVAN

MW01285748

Making Sense of
Integers

DR. RANDY PALISOC

IRONBOX®
Education

IRONBOX®
Education

Contents

Essential Background Information

Making Sense of Integers

About the Author

My name is Dr. Randy Palisoc, and I'm on a mission to give kids **Power Over Numbers** and **Power Over Learning.**

I am a former classroom teacher, and I was a founder of the **five-time national award winning** Synergy Academies, whose elementary school was named the **#1 Urban Elementary School in America** by the National Center for Urban School Transformation in 2013.

The reason I designed this system is that too many students do not have a strong foundation in math, and they do not "get" the standard explanations found in many textbooks. This is troubling because students who struggle early on are often unable catch up to their peers later in life.

On the other hand, students who do have strong foundations have a greater shot at success later in life. In 2013, for example, students who were with Synergy since elementary school (all minority students) had a 95% pass rate on the California High School Exit Exam, compared to only about 79% statewide (all ethnicities).

As shown above, **strong foundations really do matter.**

The Core Advantage math fluency system by Ironbox Education is designed to build those foundations and to build fluency as quickly and as easily as possible. It does so by thinking like kids and teaching in a way that makes sense to them.

I designed this math fluency system based on my experience working with thousands of students from elementary school through high school and finding out what makes them successful. I hope you are able to use this system to give your students or children Power Over Numbers™ and Power Over Learning™!

Dr. Randy Palisoc received his Bachelor of Science degree from the University of Southern California (USC), his Master of Education degree from the University of California, Los Angeles (UCLA), and his Doctor of Education degree from USC.

Making Sense of Integers

Understanding More of the World Around Us

So far, students have learned how to add, subtract, multiply, and divide positive numbers. However, the world is full of both positive *and* negative numbers. Consider the following:

- Temperatures can go both above zero and below zero.
- A mountain can be thousands of feet above sea level, while a submarine can go thousands of feet below sea level.
- A house can either increase or decrease in value.
- Money can be deposited into or deducted from a bank account.

This is why integers are so important – they help us understand more of the world around us.

Adding, subtracting, multiplying, and dividing integers are full of nuances, and students must pay attention to these details. This book, *Making Sense of Integers,* will help students notice these details so they can gain fluency working with integers.

How does this system work?

First things first.

Making Sense of Integers goes through the four basic operations of addition, subtraction, multiplication, and division, and it includes working with both single-digit and multi-digit integers. Therefore, please make sure students are fluent with these operations and have gone through the following books first:

- *Easy Breezy Addition & Subtraction*
- *Multi-digit Addition & Subtraction*
- *10 Powerful Steps to Multiplication Fluency*
- *Making Sense of Division*

The Core Advantage math fluency system is different from ordinary workbooks. The system is designed to have students work interactively on short, easy-to-understand guided lessons with their teacher or their parent. The reason for this is that when students (especially young students) work with an actual person, it makes learning a much more personal and meaningful experience. **The human touch matters.**

It's important for teachers or parents to watch the lesson-by-lesson demo videos. This way, they'll know the key nuances to point out, and it takes the guesswork and confusion out of the lesson. There are also fully-annotated answer keys that not only show the answer, but also show the steps involved in getting there.

Each lesson provides students with well-thought-out, purposeful practice to promote fluency, and all the lessons build systematically upon each other. The following page provides a suggested pacing plan, and you can adjust the pacing as needed.

Pacing: Making Sense of Integers

Please make sure students are fluent with the basic operations of addition, subtraction, multiplication, and division before starting this unit on integers. If students are not yet fluent, use the following books:

- *Easy Breezy Addition & Subtraction*
- *Multi-digit Addition & Subtraction*
- *10 Powerful Steps to Multiplication Fluency*
- *Making Sense of Division*

A sample pacing plan for this book is shown below, and the pacing can be adjusted as necessary.

	Monday	Tuesday	Wednesday	Thursday	Friday
Week 1	Lesson 1-1 Adding and Subtracting Integers Demo	Lesson 1-2 Adding and Subtracting Integers Lesson 2 Adding and Subtracting Integers	Lesson 3-1 Shortcut for Subtracting a Positive Integer from Another Integer	Lesson 3-2 Shortcut for Subtracting a Positive Integer from Another Integer Lesson 4-1 Multiplying and Dividing Integers Demo	Lesson 4-2 Multiplying and Dividing Integers Lesson 5-1 Adding, Subtracting, Multiplying, and Dividing Integers
Week 2	Lesson 5-2 Adding, Subtracting, Multiplying, and Dividing Integers Lesson 6-1 Adding, Subtracting, Multiplying, and Dividing Integers	Lesson 6-2 Adding, Subtracting, Multiplying, and Dividing Integers Lesson 7 Sea Level, Above Sea Level, and Below Sea Level	Lesson 8 Increases or Decreases in Temperature Lesson 9-1 Adding and Subtracting Multi-digit Numbers in Your Head	Lesson 9-2 Adding and Subtracting Multi-digit Numbers in Your Head Lesson 10 Elevation Gain or Loss	Lesson 11-1 Adding and Subtracting Multi-digit Integers
Week 3	Lesson 11-2 Adding and Subtracting Multi-digit Integers Lesson 12 Mauna Kea Temperature and Elevation	Lesson 13-1 Comparing Integers Lesson 13-2 Comparing Integers	Lesson 14-1 Comparing Integers Lesson 14-2 Comparing Integers	Lesson 15-1 Multiplying and Dividing Integers with Hanging Zeroes	Lesson 15-2 Multiplying and Dividing Integers with Hanging Zeroes
Week 4	Lesson 16-1 Adding, Subtracting, and Multiplying Integers	Lesson 16-2 Adding, Subtracting, and Multiplying Integers	Lesson 17 Integer Word Problems Involving Multiplication and Division	Lesson 18 Integer Word Problems Involving Multiplication and Division	

Making Sense of Integers | © MathFluency.com | **Teachers: Log in for demo videos.**

Addressing State Learning Standards or the Common Core State Standards

Today, schools across America are either using their own state's learning standards or the Common Core State Standards.

No matter what learning standards a school is using, this system helps give students an academic advantage by building fluency faster than has been possible in the past. Fluency is important for all students because it helps them be more precise, which in turn helps them more easily make sense of math.

Take a look at these two Standards for Mathematical Practice (MP), which are used by states using the Common Core State Standards:

MP #1: Make sense of problems and persevere in solving them.
MP #6: Attend to precision.

How do these two math practices go together?

- If students **cannot** attend to precision (#6), then they will not make sense of problems (#1), and they will not persevere in solving them (#1).

On the other hand,

- If students **can** attend to precision (#6), then they are more likely to make sense of problems (#1) and are more likely to persevere in solving them (#1).

As you can see, attending to precision (#6) can mean the difference between confidence and confusion.

The unique Core Advantage system used in this book can help give students an academic advantage in a short amount of time. It is designed to build fluency so that students can attend to precision (#6) and actually understand what they're doing in math.

It does take hard work and practice on the part of students, and only students themselves can determine their level of success based on their effort. The good news is that the greater their level of fluency, the more confidence students will have, and the more likely they are to persevere and put in that necessary hard work and practice.

Fluency matters, and I hope that you are able to use this system to build that fluency with your students.

-- Dr. Randy Palisoc

Making Sense of Integers | © MathFluency.com | **Teachers: Log in for demo videos.**

Making Sense of
Integers

Go down your **Success Tracker** in the order shown below, and write your score for each of the activities as you complete them. The goal is to make any corrections necessary to earn a score of 100%.

Lesson	Lesson Name	Score
1-1	**Adding and Subtracting Integers** Demo	
1-2	Adding and Subtracting Integers	
2	Adding and Subtracting Integers	
3-1	**Shortcut for Subtracting a Positive Integer from Another Integer**	
3-2	Shortcut for Subtracting a Positive Integer from Another Integer	
4-1	**Multiplying and Dividing Integers** Demo	
4-2	Multiplying and Dividing Integers	
5-1	**Adding, Subtracting, Multiplying, and Dividing Integers**	
5-2	Adding, Subtracting, Multiplying, and Dividing Integers	
6-1	Adding, Subtracting, Multiplying, and Dividing Integers	
6-2	Adding, Subtracting, Multiplying, and Dividing Integers	
7	Sea Level, Above Sea Level, and Below Sea Level	
8	Increases or Decreases in Temperature	
9-1	**Adding and Subtracting Multi-digit Numbers in Your Head**	
9-2	Adding and Subtracting Multi-digit Numbers in Your Head	
10	Elevation Gain or Loss	
11-1	Adding and Subtracting Multi-digit Integers	
11-2	Adding and Subtracting Multi-digit Integers	
12	Mauna Kea Temperature and Elevation	
13-1	**Comparing Integers**	
13-2	Comparing Integers	
14-1	Comparing Integers	
14-2	Comparing Integers	
15-1	Multiplying and Dividing Integers with Hanging Zeroes	
15-2	Multiplying and Dividing Integers with Hanging Zeroes	
16-1	Adding, Subtracting, and Multiplying Integers	
16-2	Adding, Subtracting, and Multiplying Integers	
17	Integer Word Problems Involving Multiplication and Division	
18	Integer Word Problems Involving Multiplication and Division	

Making Sense of Integers | © MathFluency.com | **Teachers: Log in for demo videos.**

Name_____

Lesson 1-1: Adding and Subtracting Integers Demo

Part 1: Follow along with your instructor and the demo video to complete this lesson.

- Integers include zero (____), the natural numbers such as ____, ____, and ____ , and the opposite of natural numbers, which are negative, such as _____, _____, and _____.

- When adding integers, face the _____ direction. 🦘 **+**

- When subtracting integers, face the _____ direction. **-** 🦘

— Negative

+ Positive

A.	6 + **4** =	E.	6 + **−4** =
B.	6 − **4** =	F.	6 − **−4** =
C.	−6 + **4** =	G.	−6 + **−4** =
D.	−6 − **4** =	H.	−6 − **−4** =

When adding or subtracting a **negative** number, you are jumping _____ along the number line.

Subtracting Integers

1. _____ _____ _____. (We'll learn a shortcut for this in Lesson 3.)

2. Instead, use _____ _____ to _____ _____ _____.

- With your instructor, use two strokes to change the four subtraction problems above (B, D, F, and H) into four addition problems. Lightly shade in these four problems.

- Then, draw an arrow connecting each shaded problem to the non-shaded problem that it resembles. You have just cut the number of scenarios down from _____ scenarios to only _____ scenarios.

Adding Integers (Using Zero Pairs and a Sports Analogy: Positive Team and Negative Team)

1. If the signs are the **same** (both + or both −), _____ the sign and _____ the numbers.

2. If the signs are **different,** figure out which "team" _____, then _____ the numbers.

Part 2: Follow along with your instructor to use zero pairs and a sports analogy to solve these problems.

| I. | J. | K. Use two strokes. | L. Use two strokes. |
| 3 + −5 = _____ | −3 + 5 = _____ | −3 − −5 = _____ | −3 − 5 = _____ |

Lesson 1-2: Adding and Subtracting Integers

Part 1: Draw the correct number of positives and negatives for each addition problem. Then, circle the zero pairs (if there are any), and solve each problem.

HINT: Use a sports analogy. After circling the zero pairs, figure out which "team" wins (positive team or negative team) and by how many points. Example I and II have been done for you.

Example I: (different "teams") $-4 + 3 =$ **-1**	Example II: (same "team") $-4 + -3 =$ **-7**	A. $4 + -3 =$ _____	B. $4 + 3 =$ _____
C. $5 + -2 =$ _____	D. $-5 + 2 =$ _____	E. $5 + 2 =$ _____	F. $-5 + -2 =$ _____

Part 2: These problems involve the subtraction of integers. Remember, _____ _____ _____.

Instead, use _____ _____ to _____ _____ _____. Then, solve using zero pairs.

G. $3 - -4 =$ _____	H. $3 - 4 =$ _____	I. $-3 - -4 =$ _____	J. $-3 - 4 =$ _____
K. $-5 - 2 =$ _____	L. $-5 - -2 =$ _____	M. $5 - 2 =$ _____	N. $5 - -2 =$ _____

Part 3: Solve. Remember, don't subtract integers. Instead, use two strokes to add the opposite.

O. $-2 + -4 =$ _____	P. $2 + -4 =$ _____	Q. $2 - 4 =$ _____	R. $2 - -4 =$ _____
S. $-2 - -4 =$ _____	T. $-2 + 4 =$ _____	U. $2 + 4 =$ _____	V. $-2 - 4 =$ _____

Making Sense of Integers | © MathFluency.com | **Teachers: Log in for demo videos.**

Lesson 2: Adding and Subtracting Integers

Directions: Solve. Remember not to subtract integers (we'll learn a shortcut to this in Lesson 3-1). Instead, draw two strokes and add the opposite. Be sure that negative signs are written long and clear. If necessary, use the extra space to draw positives and negatives, then use zero pairs to find your answer. ***Work carefully, and don't rush.***

Column 1

3 + −5 = _____

−3 + 5 = _____

−3 − 3 = _____

3 + 0 = _____

−3 + −5 = _____

−5 − −3 = _____

0 − −3 = _____

−3 − −3 = _____

−3 − 5 = _____

3 − −3 = _____

−3 + 3 = _____

5 + 3 = _____

5 − 3 = _____

0 + 3 = _____

3 − 0 = _____

−5 + −3 = _____

3 + 3 = _____

3 − 5 = _____

−3 − −3 = _____

−3 − 0 = _____

Column 2

0 − 3 = _____

−5 + 3 = _____

5 − −3 = _____

0 − 3 = _____

−3 − 5 = _____

3 + −3 = _____

5 + −3 = _____

−5 − 3 = _____

0 − −3 = _____

3 − −5 = _____

3 − −3 = _____

−3 − −5 = _____

3 + 5 = _____

−5 − −3 = _____

0 + −3 = _____

−5 − −3 = _____

3 − 3 = _____

−3 + −3 = _____

0 + −3 = _____

−3 + 0 = _____

Lesson 3-1: Shortcut for Subtracting a Positive Integer from Another Integer

Part 1: Follow along with your instructor to complete this lesson. All these problems involve subtracting a **positive** integer (shown in bold) from another integer (either positive or negative).

Method 1
Don't subtract integers. Draw
two strokes to add the opposite.

$3 - \mathbf{5} =$ _____

$2 - \mathbf{8} =$ _____

$7 - \mathbf{4} =$ _____

$-5 - \mathbf{7} =$ _____

$-4 - \mathbf{9} =$ _____

Method 2
Interpret the subtraction
sign (–) as a negative sign.

$3 - \mathbf{5} =$ _____

$-5 - \mathbf{7} =$ _____

$-4 - \mathbf{9} =$ _____

$2 - \mathbf{8} =$ _____

$7 - \mathbf{4} =$ _____

Subtracting Integers

The original rule was, "Don't subtract integers." Instead, draw two strokes to add the opposite.

In the comparison above, you saw that there is a shortcut for subtracting a _____ integer from another

integer, and you didn't have to draw two strokes to add the opposite. Therefore, just use this more specific rule:

- Don't subtract _____ integers. Instead, draw two strokes to add the opposite.

Part 2: Solve. Remember to use the shortcut for subtracting a **positive** integer from another integer. Also, remember, not to subtract **negative** integers. Instead, draw two strokes and add the opposite. Work carefully, and don't rush.

Column 1

$-4 - 7 =$ _____

$7 - 4 =$ _____

$-7 - 4 =$ _____

$4 - 7 =$ _____

$-4 - 4 =$ _____

$-7 - -4 =$ _____

$4 - -7 =$ _____

$-4 - -4 =$ _____

$-4 - -7 =$ _____

$7 - -4 =$ _____

Column 2

$4 - -4 =$ _____

$4 - -7 =$ _____

$-4 - -7 =$ _____

$-7 - 4 =$ _____

$-4 - -4 =$ _____

$-7 - -4 =$ _____

$-4 - 7 =$ _____

$7 - -4 =$ _____

$4 - 7 =$ _____

$7 - 4 =$ _____

Column 3

$-4 + 7 =$ _____

$0 - -4 =$ _____

$7 + 4 =$ _____

$-7 + -4 =$ _____

$0 - 4 =$ _____

$4 + -4 =$ _____

$0 - -4 =$ _____

$-7 - -4 =$ _____

$4 - 4 =$ _____

$0 + -4 =$ _____

Lesson 3-2: Shortcut for Subtracting a Positive Integer from Another Integer

Part 1: Review the two methods for subtracting a **positive** integer (shown in bold) from another integer (either positive or negative). As shown in the Lesson 3 demo video, Method 2 involves interpreting the subtraction sign (–) as a negative sign.

Method 1
Don't subtract integers. Draw
two strokes to add the opposite.

$4 - \mathbf{9} =$ _____

$5 - \mathbf{7} =$ _____

$6 - \mathbf{2} =$ _____

$-3 - \mathbf{8} =$ _____

$-2 - \mathbf{6} =$ _____

Method 2
Interpret the subtraction
sign (–) as a negative sign.

$4 - \mathbf{9} =$ _____

$6 - \mathbf{2} =$ _____

$-3 - \mathbf{8} =$ _____

$5 - \mathbf{7} =$ _____

$-2 - \mathbf{6} =$ _____

Subtracting Integers

Original Rule: "Don't subtract integers." Instead, draw two strokes to add the opposite.

More Specific Rule: Don't subtract _____ integers. Instead, draw two strokes to add the opposite.

There is a shortcut for subtracting a _____ integer. Interpret the subtraction sign (–) as a negative sign.

Part 2: Solve. Remember to use the shortcut for subtracting a **positive** integer from another integer. Also, remember, not to subtract **negative** integers. Instead, draw two strokes and add the opposite. Work carefully, and don't rush.

Column 1	Column 2	Column 3
$-9 - -5 =$ _____	$-9 - -5 =$ _____	$5 + -5 =$ _____
$5 - -9 =$ _____	$-5 - 9 =$ _____	$0 - -5 =$ _____
$-5 - -5 =$ _____	$9 - -5 =$ _____	$-9 - -5 =$ _____
$-5 - -9 =$ _____	$5 - 9 =$ _____	$5 - 5 =$ _____
$9 - -5 =$ _____	$9 - 5 =$ _____	$0 + -5 =$ _____
$-5 - 9 =$ _____	$5 - -5 =$ _____	$-5 + 9 =$ _____
$9 - 5 =$ _____	$5 - -9 =$ _____	$0 - -5 =$ _____
$-9 - 5 =$ _____	$-5 - -9 =$ _____	$9 + 5 =$ _____
$5 - 9 =$ _____	$-9 - 5 =$ _____	$-9 + -5 =$ _____
$-5 - 5 =$ _____	$-5 - -5 =$ _____	$0 - 5 =$ _____

Name_____

Lesson 4-1: Multiplying and Dividing Integers Demo

Part 1: Follow along with your instructor and with the demo video to complete this lesson.

Multiplying and dividing integers is much _____ than adding and subtracting integers.

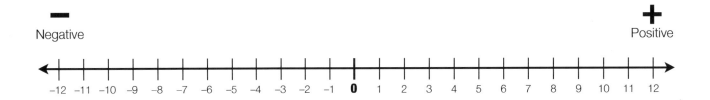

—
Negative

+
Positive

A.	3 x 4 =	+ · + =
B.	3 x −4 =	+ · − =
C.	−3 x 4 =	− · + =
D.	−3 x −4 =	− · − =

Multiplying Integers

1. _____ _____ _____ _____.

Dividing Integers

1. _____ _____ _____ _____.

Part 2: Multiply or divide.

Column 1

5 x   6 = ____

−5 x   6 = ____

−5 x −6 = ____

5 x −6 = ____

−30 ÷   5 = ____

Column 2

−6 x   5 = ____

30 ÷ −5 = ____

6 x   0 = ____

−30 ÷ −5 = ____

−6 x −5 = ____

Column 3

0 ÷ −5 = ____

6 x −5 = ____

0 x −5 = ____

−6 x   0 = ____

30 ÷   5 = ____

Lesson 4-2: Multiplying and Dividing Integers

Part 1: Review the rules for multiplying and dividing integers.

Multiplying and dividing integers is much _____ than adding and subtracting integers.

Multiplying Integers

1. _____ _____ _____ _____.

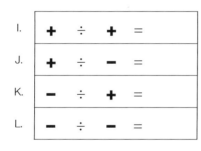

A.	**+**	·	**+**	=
B.	**+**	·	**−**	=
C.	**−**	·	**+**	=
D.	**−**	·	**−**	=

E.	**−**	·	**+**	=
F.	**−**	·	**−**	=
G.	**+**	·	**+**	=
H.	**+**	·	**−**	=

Dividing Integers

1. _____ _____ _____ _____.

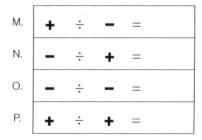

I.	**+**	÷	**+**	=
J.	**+**	÷	**−**	=
K.	**−**	÷	**+**	=
L.	**−**	÷	**−**	=

M.	**+**	÷	**−**	=
N.	**−**	÷	**+**	=
O.	**−**	÷	**−**	=
P.	**+**	÷	**+**	=

Part 2: Multiply or divide.

Column 1	Column 2	Column 3
−4 x 3 = ____	0 ÷ −3 = ____	3 x 4 = ____
12 ÷ −3 = ____	4 x −3 = ____	−3 x 4 = ____
4 x 0 = ____	0 x −3 = ____	−3 x −4 = ____
−12 ÷ −3 = ____	−4 x 0 = ____	3 x −4 = ____
−4 x −3 = ____	12 ÷ 3 = ____	−12 ÷ 3 = ____

Name_____

Lesson 5-1: Adding, Subtracting, Multiplying, and Dividing Integers

Directions: Add, subtract, multiply, or divide. This assignment covers every possible combination, so **_don't rush._** Work carefully, and focus on the signs and operations. Remember to use the shortcut for subtracting a positive integer from another integer.

Column 1

2 + −6 = ____

−2 + 6 = ____

−2 − 2 = ____

2 + 0 = ____

−2 + −6 = ____

−6 − −2 = ____

0 − −2 = ____

−2 − −2 = ____

−2 − 6 = ____

2 − −2 = ____

−4 ÷ 2 = ____

−12 ÷ −6 = ____

6 x −2 = ____

2 − −2 = ____

2 x −6 = ____

0 ÷ −2 = ____

−2 x 6 = ____

−4 ÷ −2 = ____

2 x 0 = ____

−2 x −6 = ____

6 + 2 = ____

6 − 2 = ____

0 + 2 = ____

2 − 0 = ____

−6 + −2 = ____

Column 2

12 ÷ −6 = ____

4 ÷ 2 = ____

−2 x −2 = ____

0 x −2 = ____

−2 x 0 = ____

2 + 2 = ____

2 − 6 = ____

−2 − −2 = ____

−2 − 0 = ____

2 x 2 = ____

0 − 2 = ____

−6 + 2 = ____

6 − −2 = ____

12 ÷ 2 = ____

4 ÷ −2 = ____

0 − 2 = ____

0 ÷ −2 = ____

−2 − 6 = ____

0 ÷ 2 = ____

−6 x 2 = ____

2 + −2 = ____

−12 ÷ 6 = ____

0 ÷ 2 = ____

−12 ÷ −2 = ____

2 x −2 = ____

Column 3

6 x 2 = ____

0 x 2 = ____

12 ÷ 6 = ____

0 ÷ 2 = ____

−6 x −2 = ____

−12 ÷ 2 = ____

−2 x 2 = ____

12 ÷ −2 = ____

6 + −2 = ____

−6 − 2 = ____

2 x 6 = ____

12 ÷ −6 = ____

0 − −2 = ____

0 x −2 = ____

2 − −6 = ____

−2 + 2 = ____

−2 − −6 = ____

2 + 6 = ____

−6 − −2 = ____

0 + −2 = ____

−6 − −2 = ____

2 − 2 = ____

−2 + −2 = ____

0 + −2 = ____

−2 + 0 = ____

Lesson 5-2: Adding, Subtracting, Multiplying, and Dividing Integers

Directions: Add, subtract, multiply, or divide. This assignment covers every possible combination, so **don't rush.** Work carefully, and focus on the signs and operations. Remember to use the shortcut for subtracting a positive integer from another integer.

Column 1	Column 2	Column 3
$5 + -3 =$	$15 \div -3 =$	$3 \times 5 =$
$-5 + 3 =$	$5 \div 5 =$	$0 \times 5 =$
$-5 - 5 =$	$-5 \times -5 =$	$15 \div 3 =$
$5 + 0 =$	$0 \times -5 =$	$0 \div 5 =$
$-5 + -3 =$	$-5 \times 0 =$	$-3 \times -5 =$
$-3 - -5 =$	$5 + 5 =$	$-15 \div 5 =$
$0 - -5 =$	$5 - 3 =$	$-5 \times 5 =$
$-5 - -5 =$	$-5 - -5 =$	$15 \div -5 =$
$-5 - 3 =$	$-5 - 0 =$	$3 + -5 =$
$5 - -5 =$	$5 \times 5 =$	$-3 - 5 =$
$-5 \div 5 =$	$0 - 5 =$	$5 \times 3 =$
$-15 \div -3 =$	$-3 + 5 =$	$15 \div -3 =$
$3 \times -5 =$	$3 - -5 =$	$0 - -5 =$
$5 - -5 =$	$15 \div 5 =$	$0 \times -5 =$
$5 \times -3 =$	$5 \div -5 =$	$5 - -3 =$
$0 \div -5 =$	$0 - 5 =$	$-5 + 5 =$
$-5 \times 3 =$	$0 \div -5 =$	$-5 - -3 =$
$-5 \div -5 =$	$-5 - 3 =$	$5 + 3 =$
$5 \times 0 =$	$0 \div 5 =$	$-3 - -5 =$
$-5 \times -3 =$	$-3 \times 5 =$	$0 + -5 =$
$3 + 5 =$	$5 + -5 =$	$-3 - -5 =$
$3 - 5 =$	$-15 \div 3 =$	$5 - 5 =$
$0 + 5 =$	$0 \div 5 =$	$-5 + -5 =$
$5 - 0 =$	$-15 \div -5 =$	$0 + -5 =$
$-3 + -5 =$	$5 \times -5 =$	$-5 + 0 =$

Lesson 6-1: Adding, Subtracting, Multiplying, and Dividing Integers

Directions: Add, subtract, multiply, or divide. This assignment covers every possible combination, so **don't rush.** Work carefully, and focus on the signs and operations. Remember to use the shortcut for subtracting a positive integer from another integer.

Column 1	Column 2	Column 3
$3 + -6 = $ _____	$18 \div -6 = $ _____	$6 \times 3 = $ _____
$-3 + 6 = $ _____	$9 \div 3 = $ _____	$0 \times 3 = $ _____
$-3 - 3 = $ _____	$-3 \times -3 = $ _____	$18 \div 6 = $ _____
$3 + 0 = $ _____	$0 \times -3 = $ _____	$0 \div 3 = $ _____
$-3 + -6 = $ _____	$-3 \times 0 = $ _____	$-6 \times -3 = $ _____
$-6 - -3 = $ _____	$3 + 3 = $ _____	$-18 \div 3 = $ _____
$0 - -3 = $ _____	$3 - 6 = $ _____	$-3 \times 3 = $ _____
$-3 - -3 = $ _____	$-3 - -3 = $ _____	$18 \div -3 = $ _____
$-3 - 6 = $ _____	$-3 - 0 = $ _____	$6 + -3 = $ _____
$3 - -3 = $ _____	$3 \times 3 = $ _____	$-6 - 3 = $ _____
$-9 \div 3 = $ _____	$0 - 3 = $ _____	$3 \times 6 = $ _____
$-18 \div -6 = $ _____	$-6 + 3 = $ _____	$18 \div -6 = $ _____
$6 \times -3 = $ _____	$6 - -3 = $ _____	$0 - -3 = $ _____
$3 - -3 = $ _____	$18 \div 3 = $ _____	$0 \times -3 = $ _____
$3 \times -6 = $ _____	$9 \div -3 = $ _____	$3 - -6 = $ _____
$0 \div -3 = $ _____	$0 - 3 = $ _____	$-3 + 3 = $ _____
$-3 \times 6 = $ _____	$0 \div -3 = $ _____	$-3 - -6 = $ _____
$-9 \div -3 = $ _____	$-3 - 6 = $ _____	$3 + 6 = $ _____
$3 \times 0 = $ _____	$0 \div 3 = $ _____	$-6 - -3 = $ _____
$-3 \times -6 = $ _____	$-6 \times 3 = $ _____	$0 + -3 = $ _____
$6 + 3 = $ _____	$3 + -3 = $ _____	$-6 - -3 = $ _____
$6 - 3 = $ _____	$-18 \div 6 = $ _____	$3 - 3 = $ _____
$0 + 3 = $ _____	$0 \div 3 = $ _____	$-3 + -3 = $ _____
$3 - 0 = $ _____	$-18 \div -3 = $ _____	$0 + -3 = $ _____
$-6 + -3 = $ _____	$3 \times -3 = $ _____	$-3 + 0 = $ _____

Lesson 6-2: Adding, Subtracting, Multiplying, and Dividing Integers

Directions: Add, subtract, multiply, or divide. This assignment covers every possible combination, so **don't rush.** Work carefully, and focus on the signs and operations. Remember to use the shortcut for subtracting a positive integer from another integer.

Column 1

8 + −7 = _____

−8 + 7 = _____

−8 − 8 = _____

8 + 0 = _____

−8 + −7 = _____

−7 − −8 = _____

0 − −8 = _____

−8 − −8 = _____

−8 − 7 = _____

8 − −8 = _____

−64 ÷ 8 = _____

−56 ÷ −7 = _____

7 x −8 = _____

8 − −8 = _____

8 x −7 = _____

0 ÷ −8 = _____

−8 x 7 = _____

−64 ÷ −8 = _____

8 x 0 = _____

−8 x −7 = _____

7 + 8 = _____

7 − 8 = _____

0 + 8 = _____

8 − 0 = _____

−7 + −8 = _____

Column 2

56 ÷ −7 = _____

64 ÷ 8 = _____

−8 x −8 = _____

0 x −8 = _____

−8 x 0 = _____

8 + 8 = _____

8 − 7 = _____

−8 − −8 = _____

−8 − 0 = _____

8 x 8 = _____

0 − 8 = _____

−7 + 8 = _____

7 − −8 = _____

56 ÷ 8 = _____

64 ÷ −8 = _____

0 − 8 = _____

0 ÷ −8 = _____

−8 − 7 = _____

0 ÷ 8 = _____

−7 x 8 = _____

8 + −8 = _____

−56 ÷ 7 = _____

0 ÷ 8 = _____

−56 ÷ −8 = _____

8 x −8 = _____

Column 3

7 x 8 = _____

0 x 8 = _____

56 ÷ 7 = _____

0 ÷ 8 = _____

−7 x −8 = _____

−56 ÷ 8 = _____

−8 x 8 = _____

56 ÷ −8 = _____

7 + −8 = _____

−7 − 8 = _____

8 x 7 = _____

56 ÷ −7 = _____

0 − −8 = _____

0 x −8 = _____

8 − −7 = _____

−8 + 8 = _____

−8 − −7 = _____

8 + 7 = _____

−7 − −8 = _____

0 + −8 = _____

−7 − −8 = _____

8 − 8 = _____

−8 + −8 = _____

0 + −8 = _____

−8 + 0 = _____

Lesson 7: Sea Level, Above Sea Level, and Below Sea Level

Directions: Using integers and feet, label the **elevation or depth** of the objects in the diagram. Then, in each problem, find how much higher the first object is located compared to the second object (measured in feet).

A. elevation of palm tree vs. depth of fish _____ ___ _____ = _____	B. depth of fish vs. depth of sea star _____ ___ _____ = _____	C. depth of sailboat vs. depth of sea star _____ ___ _____ = _____
D. elevation of shovel/pail vs. depth of fish _____ ___ _____ = _____	E. elevation of palm tree vs. elevation of shovel/pail _____ ___ _____ = _____	F. depth of beach ball vs. depth of sailboat _____ ___ _____ = _____
G. object with the highest elevation vs. object with the greatest depth _____ ___ _____ = _____	H. elevation of shovel/pail vs. depth of sea star _____ ___ _____ = _____	I. height of the sailboat from the top of the mast to the bottom of the keel _____ ___ _____ = _____

Definitions

Sea Level: the average height of the ocean's surface
Elevation: the height above sea level
Depth: the distance below sea level

Elevations and Depths

beach ball: floating at sea level (0 feet)
sailboat: floating at sea level
shovel and pail: 3 ft above sea level
palm tree: 8 ft above sea level
fish: 4 ft below sea level
sea star: sitting on the ocean floor, 8 ft below the surface

Information for Problem I Only

sailboat's mast: 7 ft above sea level
sailboat's keel: 2 ft below the surface

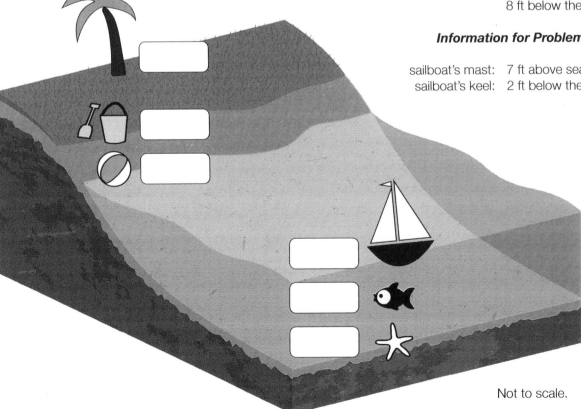

Not to scale.

Lesson 8: Increases or Decreases in Temperature

Directions: On a mountain summit, the following temperatures were recorded over a 24-hour period from midnight Monday to midnight Tuesday. Write the temperature at the times shown, and indicate whether the temperature got warmer, colder, or stayed the same from one time period to the next. Find the increase or decrease in temperature.

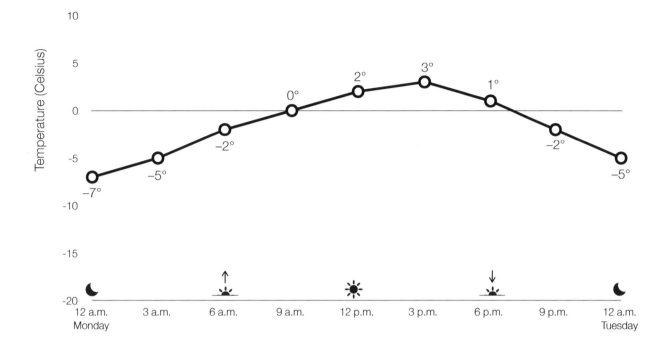

Example:	A.	B.
3 p.m. → 9 p.m.	9 p.m. → 12 a.m. (Tue.)	3 a.m. → 3 p.m.
3° → −2° colder	____ → ____ _____	____ → ____ _____
Finish the rest of this example with your instructor.		
−2 − 3 = ____	____ ____ ____ = _____	____ ____ ____ = _____
C.	D.	E.
12 p.m. → 3 p.m.	6 a.m. → 9 p.m.	3 p.m. → 6 p.m.
____ → ____ _____	____ → ____ _____	____ → ____ _____
____ ____ ____ = _____	____ ____ ____ = _____	____ ____ ____ = _____
F.	G.	H.
12 p.m. → 9 p.m.	3 a.m. → 9 a.m.	lowest → highest temperature
____ → ____ _____	____ → ____ _____	____ → ____ _____
____ ____ ____ = _____	____ ____ ____ = _____	____ ____ ____ = _____

Name_____

Lesson 9-1: Adding and Subtracting Multi-digit Numbers in Your Head

The next set of lessons involve adding and subtracting multi-digit integers. In order to save you time, it will help if you are able to do some of these problems in your head. Adding and subtracting multi-digit numbers in your head was covered in the book *Multi-digit Addition & Subtraction*. This lesson provides a review.

Part 1: Use **Stepping Stones** to find the difference in your head. Use the hint if necessary.

A.	B.	C.
23 − 14 = ____	101 − 93 = ____	165 − 93 = ____
Stepping Stone: 20	Stepping Stone: 100	Stepping Stone: 100
Think: ____ + ____ = ____	Think: ____ + ____ = ____	Think: ____ + ____ = ____
D.	E.	F.
101 − 34 = ____	93 − 34 = ____	65 − 28 = ____
Stepping Stone: 100	Stepping Stones: 40 and 90	Stepping Stones: 30 and 60
Think: ____ + ____ = ____	____ + ____ + ____ = ____	____ + ____ + ____ = ____

Part 2: Use the standard algorithm to find the difference in your head. These problems do not involve regrouping.

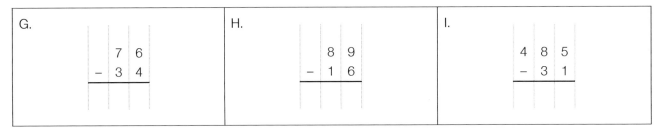

G.	H.	I.
7 6 − 3 4	8 9 − 1 6	4 8 5 − 3 1

Part 3: Find the sums in your head.

J.	K.	L.	M.
800 + 40 + 2 = _____	140 + 10 + 6 = _____	140 + 16 = _____	110 + 15 = _____

Part 4: Find the sum in your head (add the place values from **left to right**).

N.	O.	P.	Q.
23 + 34 = _____	14 + 34 = _____	93 + 14 = _____	165 + 23 = _____
Think: _____ + ____	Think: _____ + ____	Think: _____ + ____	Think: ____ + ____ + ____
R.	S.	T.	U.
67 + 8**9** = _____	89 + 58 = _____	26 + 87 = _____	78 + 47 = _____
Think: _____ + ____	Think: _____ + _____	Think: _____ + ____	Think: _____ + ____

Lesson 9-2: Adding and Subtracting Multi-digit Numbers in Your Head

The next set of lessons involve adding and subtracting multi-digit integers. In order to save you time, it will help if you are able to do some of these problems in your head. Adding and subtracting multi-digit numbers in your head was covered in the book *Multi-digit Addition & Subtraction.* This lesson provides a review.

Part 1: Use **Stepping Stones** to find the difference in your head. Use the hint if necessary.

A.	B.	C.
85 – 77 = ____	106 – 97 = ____	182 – 95 = ____
Stepping Stone: 80	Stepping Stone: 100	Stepping Stone: 100
Think: ____ + ____ = ____	Think: ____ + ____ = ____	Think: ____ + _____ = _____
D.	E.	F.
106 – 48 = ____	73 – 47 = ____	84 – 67 = ____
Stepping Stone: 100	Stepping Stones: 50 and 70	Stepping Stones: 70 and 80
Think: _____ + ____ = _____	____ + _____ + ____ = _____	____ + _____ + ____ = _____

Part 2: Use the standard algorithm to find the difference in your head. These problems do not involve regrouping.

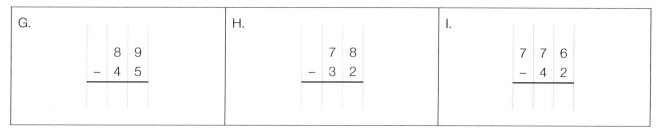

G.	H.	I.
8 9 – 4 5	7 8 – 3 2	7 7 6 – 4 2

Part 3: Find the sums in your head.

J.	K.	L.	M.
270 + 10 + 3 = _____	270 + 13 = _____	130 + 19 = _____	450 + 17 = _____

Part 4: Find the sum in your head (add the place values from **left to right**).

N.	O.	P.	Q.
35 + **4**3 = _____	56 + 42 = _____	84 + 24 = _____	453 + 46 = _____
Think: _____ + ____	Think: _____ + ____	Think: _____ + ____	Think: ____ + ____ + ____
R.	S.	T.	U.
74 + **9**8 = _____	37 + 46 = _____	65 + 48 = _____	89 + 84 = _____
Think: _____ + ____	Think: _____ + ____	Think: _____ + ____	Think: _____ + ____

Lesson 10: Elevation Gain or Loss

Directions: Write the elevation at each point. Indicate whether the elevation got higher or lower from one point to the next. Find the elevation gain or loss.

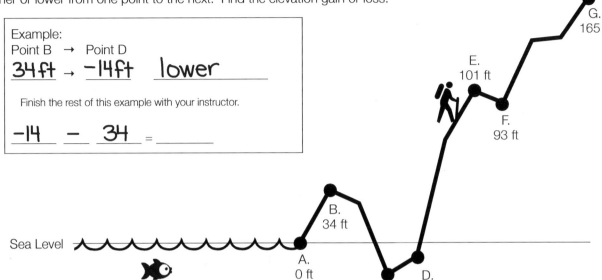

Example:
Point B → Point D

34 ft → **−14 ft**   **lower**

Finish the rest of this example with your instructor.

−14 − 34 = _____

Sea Level

B. 34 ft

A. 0 ft

C. −23 ft

D. −14 ft

E. 101 ft

F. 93 ft

G. 165 ft

---

1. Point A → Point B _____ → _____ _____ _____ − _____ = _____	2. Point B → Point C _____ → _____ _____ _____ − _____ = _____
3. Point C → Point D _____ → _____ _____ _____ − _____ = _____	4. Point D → Point E _____ → _____ _____ _____ − _____ = _____
5. Point E → Point F _____ → _____ _____ _____ − _____ = _____	6. Point F → Point G _____ → _____ _____ _____ − _____ = _____
7. Point D → Point F _____ → _____ _____ _____ − _____ = _____	8. lowest → highest point _____ → _____ _____ _____ − _____ = _____

Lesson 11-1: Adding and Subtracting Multi-digit Integers

Directions: Solve. Only the signs and operations change from problem to problem in each set. Use the workspace to perform your calculations.

Set 1

Workspace

A.	47 + 84 =	
B.	47 − 84 =	
C.	−47 + 84 =	
D.	−47 − 84 =	

E.	47 + −84 =	
F.	47 − −84 =	
G.	−47 + −84 =	
H.	−47 − −84 =	

Set 2

Workspace

I.	573 + 3,238 =
J.	573 − 3,238 =
K.	−573 + 3,238 =
L.	−573 − 3,238 =
M.	573 + −3,238 =
N.	573 − −3,238 =
O.	−573 + −3,238 =
P.	−573 − −3,238 =

Set 3

Workspace

Q.	−5,347 − −4,759 =
R.	−5,347 − 4,759 =
S.	5,347 − −4,759 =
T.	5,347 − 4,759 =
U.	−5,347 + −4,759 =
V.	5,347 + −4,759 =
W.	5,347 + 4,759 =
X.	−5,347 + 4,759 =

Lesson 11-2: Adding and Subtracting Multi-digit Integers

Directions: Solve. Only the signs and operations change from problem to problem in each set. Use the workspace to perform your calculations.

Set 1   Workspace

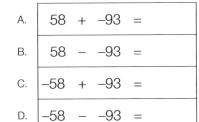

A.	58	+	−93	=
B.	58	−	−93	=
C.	−58	+	−93	=
D.	−58	−	−93	=

E.	58	+	93	=
F.	58	−	93	=
G.	−58	+	93	=
H.	−58	−	93	=

Set 2   Workspace

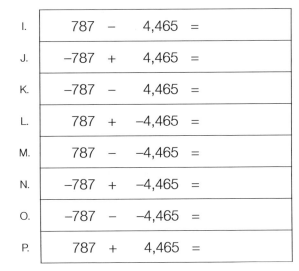

I.	787	−	4,465	=
J.	−787	+	4,465	=
K.	−787	−	4,465	=
L.	787	+	−4,465	=
M.	787	−	−4,465	=
N.	−787	+	−4,465	=
O.	−787	−	−4,465	=
P.	787	+	4,465	=

Set 3   Workspace

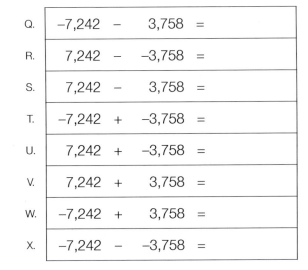

Q.	−7,242	−	3,758	=
R.	7,242	−	−3,758	=
S.	7,242	−	3,758	=
T.	−7,242	+	−3,758	=
U.	7,242	+	−3,758	=
V.	7,242	+	3,758	=
W.	−7,242	+	3,758	=
X.	−7,242	−	−3,758	=

Lesson 12: Mauna Kea Temperature and Elevation

Directions: Solve each problem. Note: Ordinarily, water freezes at 0° Celsius (32° Fahrenheit).

The summit of Mauna Kea volcano is not only *highest* location in the state of Hawaii, it is also the *coldest*.

- Record high temperature: 24° Celsius (75° Fahrenheit)
- Record low temperature: −11° Celsius (12° Fahrenheit)

A. Find the difference between the record high temperature and the record low temperature at Mauna Kea. Measure in degrees **Celsius.**	B. Find the difference between the record high temperature and the record low temperature at Mauna Kea. Measure in degrees **Fahrenheit.**

Hilo is a warm ocean town that is a two-hour drive from the frigid Mauna Kea summit. These are average temperatures for Hilo and Mauna Kea in the month of March.

- Hilo's average high temperature in March: 24° C (75° F)
- Mauna Kea's average low temperature in March :   −4° C (25° F)

C. Find the difference between Hilo's average high temperature and Mauna Kea's average low temperature. Measure in degrees **Celsius.**	D. Find the difference between Hilo's average high temperature and Mauna Kea's average low temperature. Measure in degrees **Fahrenheit.**

Mauna Kea is the tallest volcano on the Big Island of Hawaii. Mauna Kea's elevation measured from sea level is 13,803 feet. However, Mauna Kea is actually much taller than that because most of Mauna Kea is hidden below sea level. The base of Mauna Kea is 19,297 feet below sea level.

E. How tall is Mauna Kea measured from its base to its summit?

Mauna Kea Summit
13,803 feet

Big Island of Hawaii

Hilo Bay
sea level

ocean floor
−19,297 feet

Not to scale.

Lesson 13-1: Comparing Integers

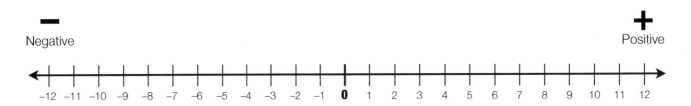

− Negative

+ Positive

Part 1: Use the number line above to put the following integers in order from least to greatest.

A.	B.
4, −4, 0, 7, −7	0, 8, 2, −8, −2
_____, _____, _____, _____, _____	_____, _____, _____, _____, _____
C.	**D.**
0, 3, −6, −9, 12	−2, 4, −6, 8, 0
_____, _____, _____, _____, _____	_____, _____, _____, _____, _____
E.	**F.**
−4, −8, −12, 4, 0	0, 7, 3, 5, −1
_____, _____, _____, _____, _____	_____, _____, _____, _____, _____

Part 2: Use the symbols greater than (>) or less than (<) to compare integers. Slow down and work carefully.

- Positive integers are always greater than negative integers.
- If both numbers are negative, the number closer to zero is bigger.

G.	H.	I.	J.
5 ___ 3	−5 ___ 3	5 ___ −3	−5 ___ −3
K.	**L.**	**M.**	**N.**
3 ___ 5	−3 ___ 5	3 ___ −5	−3 ___ −5
O.	**P.**	**Q.**	**R.**
5 ___ 0	−5 ___ 0	0 ___ 5	0 ___ −5

Lesson 13-2: Comparing Integers

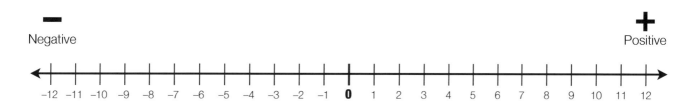

Part 1: Use the number line above to put the following integers in order from least to greatest.

A.	B.
5, −5, 0, 3, −3	0, 10, 4, −10, −4
_____, _____, _____, _____, _____	_____, _____, _____, _____, _____
C.	D.
0, 1, −3, −5, 7	4, 8, 12, −4, 0
_____, _____, _____, _____, _____	_____, _____, _____, _____, _____
E.	F.
−3, 6, 9, −12, 0	0, −8, 6, 4, −2
_____, _____, _____, _____, _____	_____, _____, _____, _____, _____

Part 2: Use the symbols greater than (>) or less than (<) to compare integers. Slow down and work carefully.

- Positive integers are always greater than negative integers.
- If both numbers are negative, the number closer to zero is bigger.

G.	H.	I.	J.
−8 ___ −6	8 ___ −6	8 ___ 6	−8 ___ 6
K.	L.	M.	N.
6 ___ −8	−6 ___ −8	6 ___ 8	−6 ___ 8
O.	P.	Q.	R.
0 ___ 8	0 ___ −8	8 ___ 0	−8 ___ 0

Lesson 14-1: Comparing Integers

Negative   Positive

−12 −11 −10 −9 −8 −7 −6 −5 −4 −3 −2 −1 0 1 2 3 4 5 6 7 8 9 10 11 12

Part 1: Put the following integers in order from least to greatest.

A.	B.
245, 8, −245, −8, 0	625, −625, 10, −10, 0
_____, _____, _____, _____, _____	_____, _____, _____, _____, _____

C.	D.
0, 1, −10, −100, 1000	2, −4, 8, 16, −32
_____, _____, _____, _____, _____	_____, _____, _____, _____, _____

E.	F.
−5, −6, −7, −8, 0	9, 10, 11, −12, −13
_____, _____, _____, _____, _____	_____, _____, _____, _____, _____

Part 2: Use the symbols greater than (>) or less than (<) to compare integers. Slow down and work carefully.

- Positive integers are always greater than negative integers.
- If both numbers are negative, the number closer to zero is bigger.

G.	H.	I.	J.
−45 ___ 2	−45 ___ −2	45 ___ −2	45 ___ 2

K.	L.	M.	N.
2 ___ 45	−2 ___ 45	−2 ___ −45	2 ___ −45

O.	P.	Q.	R.
−45 ___ 0	0 ___ 45	0 ___ −45	45 ___ 0

Lesson 14-2: Comparing Integers

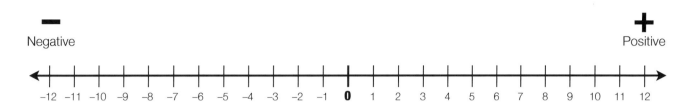

Part 1: Put the following integers in order from least to greatest.

A. 732, −6, −732, 0, 6 _____ , _____ , _____ , _____ , _____	B. 459, −459, 460, −460, 0 _____ , _____ , _____ , _____ , _____
C. −3, 9, −27, −81, 243 _____ , _____ , _____ , _____ , _____	D. 0, 10, −10, −100, 100 _____ , _____ , _____ , _____ , _____
E. 0, −9, −10, −11, −12 _____ , _____ , _____ , _____ , _____	F. −1, −2, −3, 4, 5 _____ , _____ , _____ , _____ , _____

Part 2: Use the symbols greater than (>), less than (<), or equals (=) to compare integers. Slow down and don't rush.

- Positive integers are always greater than negative integers.
- If both numbers are negative, the number closer to zero is bigger.

G. −36 ___ 36	H. −36 ___ −36	I. 36 ___ −36	J. 36 ___ 36
K. 36 ___ −36	L. 36 ___ 36	M. −36 ___ −36	N. −36 ___ 36
O. 36 ___ 0	P. 0 ___ −36	Q. 0 ___ 36	R. −36 ___ 0

Lesson 15-1: Multiplying and Dividing Integers with Hanging Zeroes

Part 1: Follow along with your instructor to multiply numbers with hanging zeroes.

A.	B.	C.	D.
$\begin{array}{r} 3 \\ \times\ 8 \\ \hline \end{array}$	$\begin{array}{r} 3\ \ 0 \\ \times\ \ \ 8 \\ \hline \end{array}$	$\begin{array}{r} 3\ \ 0\ \ 0 \\ \times\ \ \ \ \ 8 \\ \hline \end{array}$	$3 \times 8 = $ _____ $30 \times 8 = $ _____ $300 \times 8 = $ _____ $30 \times 80 = $ _____

Part 2: Follow along with your instructor to divide numbers with hanging zeroes.

E.	F.	G.	H.
$7\overline{)4\ \ 2}$	$7\overline{)4\ \ 2\ \ 0}$	$7\overline{)4\ \ 2\ \ 0\ \ 0}$	$42 \div 7 = $ _____ $420 \div 7 = $ _____ $4{,}200 \div 7 = $ _____ $4{,}200 \div 70 = $ _____
I.	J.	K.	L. Careful!
$5\overline{)2\ \ 0}$	$5\overline{)2\ \ 0\ \ 0}$	$5\overline{)2\ \ 0\ \ 0\ \ 0}$	$20 \div 5 = $ _____ $200 \div 5 = $ _____ $2{,}000 \div 5 = $ _____

Part 3: Multiply or divide.

Column 1	Column 2	Column 3
$5 \times 6 = $ _____	$-6 \times 50 = $ _____	$0 \div -5 = $ _____
$-500 \times 6 = $ _____	$3{,}000 \div -5 = $ _____	$60 \times -5 = $ _____
$-5 \times -60 = $ _____	$60 \times 0 = $ _____	$0 \times -50 = $ _____
$50 \times -60 = $ _____	$-30 \div -5 = $ _____	$-60 \times 0 = $ _____
$-300 \div 5 = $ _____	$-60 \times -50 = $ _____	$300 \div 5 = $ _____

Making Sense of Integers | © MathFluency.com | **Teachers: Log in for demo videos.**

Lesson 15-2: Multiplying and Dividing Integers with Hanging Zeroes

Part 1: Follow along with your instructor to multiply numbers with hanging zeroes.

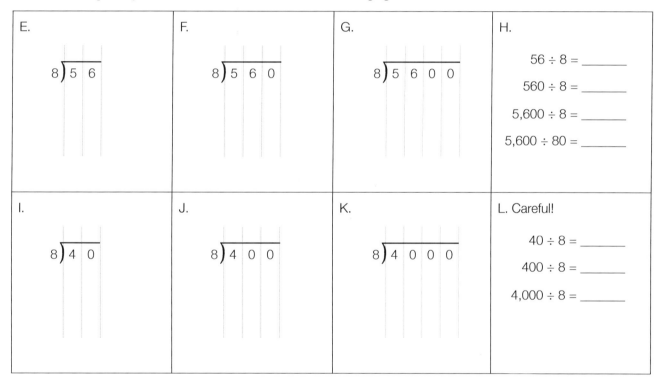

A.

```
    4
x   5
```

B.

```
  4 0
x   5
```

C.

```
4 0 0
x   5
```

D.

4 x 5 = _____

40 x 5 = _____

400 x 5 = _____

40 x 50 = _____

Part 2: Follow along with your instructor to divide numbers with hanging zeroes.

E.

8) 5 6

F.

8) 5 6 0

G.

8) 5 6 0 0

H.

56 ÷ 8 = _____

560 ÷ 8 = _____

5,600 ÷ 8 = _____

5,600 ÷ 80 = _____

I.

8) 4 0

J.

8) 4 0 0

K.

8) 4 0 0 0

L. Careful!

40 ÷ 8 = _____

400 ÷ 8 = _____

4,000 ÷ 8 = _____

Part 3: Multiply or divide.

Column 1

0 ÷ −6 = _____

70 x −6 = _____

0 x −60 = _____

−70 x 0 = _____

420 ÷ 6 = _____

Column 2

6 x 7 = _____

−600 x 7 = _____

−6 x −70 = _____

60 x −70 = _____

−420 ÷ 6 = _____

Column 3

−7 x 60 = _____

4,200 ÷ −6 = _____

70 x 0 = _____

−42 ÷ −6 = _____

−70 x −60 = _____

Lesson 16-1: Adding, Subtracting, and Multiplying Integers

Part 1: Follow along with your instructor to complete this lesson. Look for Tens, Doubles, and sums or differences that cancel each other out. Remember to use the shortcut for subtracting a positive integer from another integer.

Column 1

2 + 4 + 6 = _____

2 + 4 − 6 = _____

2 − 4 + 6 = _____

2 − 4 − 6 = _____

−2 + 4 + 6 = _____

−2 + 4 − 6 = _____

−2 − 4 + 6 = _____

−2 − 4 − 6 = _____

2 + −4 + 6 = _____

2 + −4 − 6 = _____

2 − −4 + 6 = _____

2 − −4 − 6 = _____

2 + 4 + −6 = _____

2 + 4 − −6 = _____

−2 − 4 − 6 = _____

Column 2

2 − 4 + −6 = _____

2 − 4 − −6 = _____

−2 + −4 + 6 = _____

−2 + −4 − 6 = _____

−2 − −4 + 6 = _____

−2 − −4 − 6 = _____

−2 + 4 + −6 = _____

−2 + 4 − −6 = _____

−2 − 4 + −6 = _____

−2 − 4 − −6 = _____

−2 + −4 + −6 = _____

−2 + −4 − −6 = _____

−2 − −4 + −6 = _____

−2 − −4 − −6 = _____

−2 + 4 − −6 = _____

Part 2: Multiply. Remember that when multiplying integers, two negatives will cancel each other out and give you a positive.

Column 1

2 x 4 x 6 = _____

−2 x 4 x 6 = _____

−2 x 4 x −6 = _____

2 x 4 x −6 = _____

−2 x −4 x −6 = _____

Column 2

−2 x −4 x 6 = _____

2 x −4 x −6 = _____

2 x −4 x 6 = _____

−2 x −4 x −6 = _____

2 x −4 x −6 = _____

Lesson 16-2: Adding, Subtracting, and Multiplying Integers

Part 1: Follow along with your instructor to complete this lesson. Look for Hundreds, Doubles, and sums or differences that cancel each other out. Remember to use the shortcut for subtracting a positive integer from another integer.

Column 1

25 − −50 + 75 = _____

25 − −50 − 75 = _____

25 + 50 + −75 = _____

25 + 50 − −75 = _____

−25 − 50 − 75 = _____

25 + 50 + 75 = _____

25 + 50 − 75 = _____

25 − 50 + 75 = _____

25 − 50 − 75 = _____

−25 + 50 + 75 = _____

−25 + 50 − 75 = _____

−25 − 50 + 75 = _____

−25 − 50 − 75 = _____

25 + −50 + 75 = _____

25 + −50 − 75 = _____

Column 2

−25 + −50 + −75 = _____

−25 + −50 − −75 = _____

−25 − −50 + −75 = _____

−25 − −50 − −75 = _____

−25 + 50 − −75 = _____

25 − 50 + −75 = _____

25 − 50 − −75 = _____

−25 + −50 + 75 = _____

−25 + −50 − 75 = _____

−25 − −50 + 75 = _____

−25 − −50 − 75 = _____

−25 + 50 + −75 = _____

−25 + 50 − −75 = _____

−25 − 50 + −75 = _____

−25 − 50 − −75 = _____

Part 2: Multiply. Remember that when multiplying integers, two negatives will cancel each other out and give you a positive.

Column 1

1 · 2 · 3 · 4 = _____

1 · −2 · −3 · 4 = _____

1 · 2 · 3 · −4 = _____

−1 · 2 · −3 · −4 = _____

−1 · −2 · −3 · −4 = _____

Column 2

−1 · 2 · −3 · 4 = _____

−1 · −2 · −3 · −4 = _____

1 · −2 · −3 · −4 = _____

1 · −2 · 3 · 4 = _____

0 · −1 · −2 · −3 = _____

Name_____

Lesson 17: Integer Word Problems Involving Multiplication and Division

Directions: In the first two problems in each row, write the integer and the units represented by each problem. Then, solve the last problem in each row by multiplying or dividing. ***Remember to include the units in both your calculations and in the final answer.***

Example A1. Three gallons of water are emptied from a tank. __−3 gallons__	**Example A2.** Three gallons of water are added to a tank. __3 gallons__	**Example A3.** Three gallons of water are emptied from a tank every day. Show the gain or loss in water after five days. $\dfrac{-3\,gal}{day} \cdot 5\,days = -15\,gal$
Example B1. A store has revenues of $420. __420 dollars__	**Example B2.** A store has an expense of $420. __−420 dollars__	**Example B3.** A store pays off a $420 expense over a six-month period with equal payments. Show the increase or decrease in cash per month. $\dfrac{-\$420}{6\,mo} = \dfrac{-\$70}{mo}$
C1. $7 is deposited into a bank account. ____ _____	**C2.** $7 is deducted from a bank account. ____ _____	**C3.** $7 is deposited into a bank account every month. Show the increase or decrease in the account balance after twelve months.
D1. A man loses two pounds. ____ _____	**D2.** A man gains two pounds. ____ _____	**D3.** A man loses two pounds each week. Show the increase or decrease in weight after six weeks.
E1. A quarterback in a football game gains 15 yards. ____ _____	**E2.** A quarterback loses 15 yards. ____ _____	**E3.** A quarterback loses 15 yards in three plays. Show the average loss per play.

Lesson 18: Integer Word Problems Involving Multiplication and Division

Directions: In the first two problems in each row, write the integer and the units represented by each problem. Then, solve the last problem in each row by multiplying or dividing. **Remember to include the units in both your calculations and in the final answer.**

A1. A house increases in value by $16,000. _____ _____	A2. A house decreases in value by $16,000. _____ _____	A3. A house increases in value by $16,000 over four years. Show the average gain or loss per year.
B1. A running back in a football game loses 6 yards. _____ _____	B2. A running back gains 6 yards. _____ _____	B3. A running back gains 6 yards per carry. Show the gain after three carries.
C1. $54 is deducted from a bank account. _____ _____	C2. $54 is deposited into a bank account. _____ _____	C3. $54 is deducted from an account over the course of six months. Show the increase or decrease in the account balance per month.
D1. A weightlifter gains 12 pounds. _____ _____	D2. A weightlifter loses 12 pounds. _____ _____	D3. A weightlifter wants to gain 12 lbs. of muscle in four months. Show the needed increase or decrease in weight per month.
E1. A store has revenues of $800 in cash. _____ _____	E2. A store has an expense of $800. _____ _____	E3. A store has revenues of $800 in cash per day. Show the increase or decrease in cash after seven days.

Making Sense of Integers | © MathFluency.com | **Teachers: Log in for demo videos.**

Answer Keys and Correcting Student Work

The answer keys in this section are fully annotated. They not only show the correct answer, but also how to get there. This makes is easier to troubleshoot student errors so that they can correct them.

Provide immediate feedback so that students know how they are doing. Take a look at the sample work below.

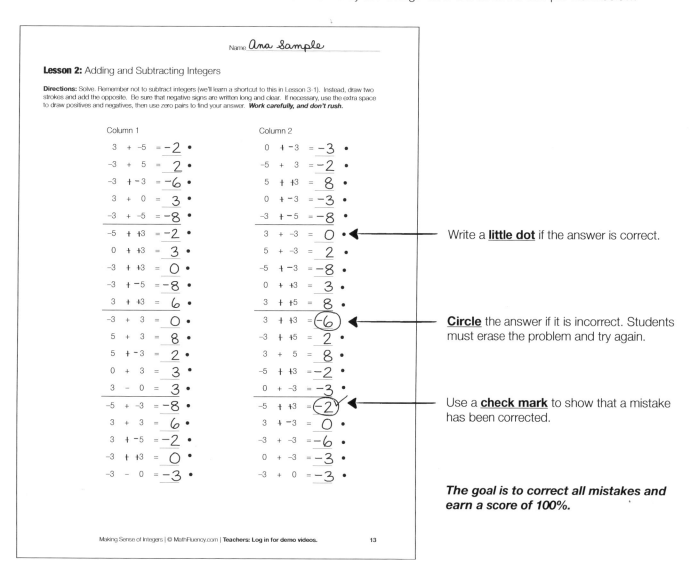

Lesson 1-1: Adding and Subtracting Integers Demo

Part 1: Follow along with your instructor and the demo video to complete this lesson.

- Integers include zero (0), the natural numbers such as 1, 2, and 3, and the opposite of natural numbers, which are negative, such as -1, -2, and -3.
- When adding integers, face the **positive** direction.
- When subtracting integers, face the **negative** direction.

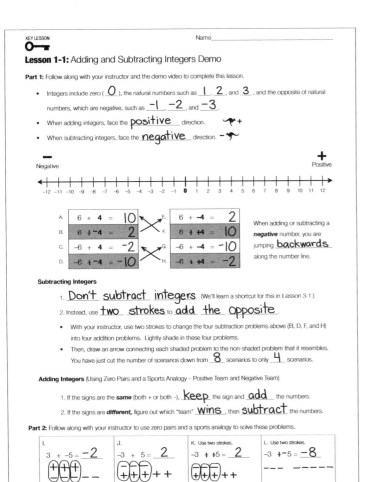

Key Points from Demo Video – Lesson 1-1
Adding and Subtracting Integers Demo

The demo video uses a kangaroo jumping along a number line to show students what happens when you add and subtract positive and negative integers. **Note: Kangaroos can't really jump backwards in real life.** This is just for demonstration purposes.

When adding integers, face the positive direction on the number line. When subtracting integers, face the negative direction.

Students should fill out the chart (Boxes A-H) as the demo is being conducted.

As shown in the demo, when you add or subtract a **negative** number, you are jumping backwards along the number line, and this can lead to confusion. For example, even if you are *facing* the positive direction, you will still end up in negative territory if you also *jump backwards*. Boxes A-H show the 8 possible scenarios when adding or subtracting integers.

To simplify this, don't subtract integers. Instead, use **two strokes** to add the opposite. This cuts down the number of scenarios from 8 to 4. Then, use zero pairs and the sports analogy of a "positive team" and a "negative team" to add the integers.

Lesson 1-2: Adding and Subtracting Integers

Part 1: Draw the correct number of positives and negatives for each addition problem. Then, circle the zero pairs (if there are any), and solve each problem.

HINT: Use a sports analogy. After circling the zero pairs, figure out which "team" wins (positive team or negative team) and by how many points. Example I and II have been done for you.

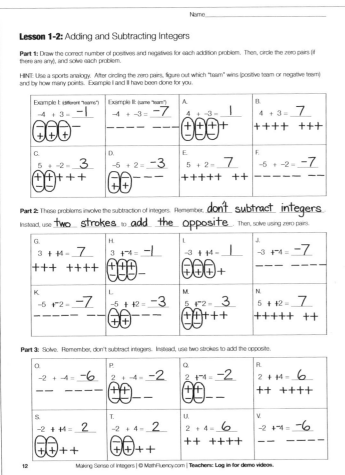

Additional Practice – Lesson 1-2
Adding and Subtracting Integers

Lesson 1-2 provides students additional practice working with zero pairs and the sports analogy of a "positive team" and a "negative team" to make sense of adding integers.

As in the previous lesson, remember not to subtract integers **(we'll learn a shortcut for this in Lesson 3-1)**. Instead, use **two strokes** to add the opposite.

Lesson 2: Adding and Subtracting Integers

Directions: Solve. Remember not to subtract integers (we'll learn a shortcut to this in Lesson 3-1). Instead, draw two strokes and add the opposite. Be sure that negative signs are written long and clear. If necessary, use the extra space to draw positives and negatives, then use zero pairs to find your answer. **Work carefully, and don't rush.**

Column 1

$3 + -5 = -2$
$-3 + 5 = 2$
$-3 + -3 = -6$
$3 + 0 = 3$
$-3 + -5 = -8$
$-5 + +3 = -2$
$0 + +3 = 3$
$-3 + +3 = 0$
$-3 + -5 = -8$
$3 + +3 = 6$
$-3 + 3 = 0$
$5 + 3 = 8$
$5 + -3 = 2$
$0 + 3 = 3$
$3 - 0 = 3$
$-5 + -3 = -8$
$3 + 3 = 6$
$3 + -5 = -2$
$-3 + +3 = 0$
$-3 - 0 = -3$

Column 2

$0 + -3 = -3$
$-5 + 3 = -2$
$5 + +3 = 8$
$0 + -3 = -3$
$-3 + -5 = -8$
$3 + -3 = 0$
$5 + -3 = 2$
$-5 + -3 = -8$
$0 + +3 = 3$
$3 + +5 = 8$
$3 + +3 = 6$
$-3 + +5 = 2$
$3 + 5 = 8$
$-5 + +3 = -2$
$0 + -3 = -3$
$-5 + +3 = -2$
$3 + -3 = 0$
$-3 + -3 = -6$
$0 + -3 = -3$
$-3 + 0 = -3$

KEY LESSON

Lesson 3-1: Shortcut for Subtracting a Positive Integer from Another Integer

Part 1: Follow along with your instructor to complete this lesson. All these problems involve subtracting a **positive** integer (shown in bold) from another integer (either positive or negative).

Method 1
Don't subtract integers. Draw two strokes to add the opposite.

$3 + -5 = -2$
$2 + -8 = -6$
$7 + -4 = 3$
$-5 + -7 = -12$
$-4 + -9 = -13$

Method 2
Interpret the subtraction sign (–) as a negative sign.

$3 - 5 = -2$
$-5 - 7 = -12$
$-4 - 9 = -13$
$2 - 8 = -6$
$7 - 4 = 3$

Subtracting Integers

The original rule was, "Don't subtract integers." Instead, draw two strokes to add the opposite.

In the comparison above, you saw that there is a shortcut for subtracting a **positive** integer from another integer, and you didn't have to draw two strokes to add the opposite. Therefore, just use this more specific rule:

• Don't subtract **negative** integers. Instead, draw two strokes to add the opposite.

Part 2: Solve. Remember to use the shortcut for subtracting a **positive** integer from another integer. Also, remember not to subtract **negative** integers. Instead, draw two strokes and add the opposite. Work carefully, and don't rush.

Column 1

$-4 - 7 = -11$
$7 - 4 = 3$
$-7 - 4 = -11$
$4 - 7 = -3$
$-4 - 4 = -8$
$-7 + +4 = -3$
$4 + +7 = 11$
$-4 + +4 = 0$
$-4 + +7 = 3$
$7 + +4 = 11$

Column 2

$4 + +4 = 8$
$4 + +7 = 11$
$-4 + +7 = 3$
$-7 - 4 = -11$
$-4 + +4 = 0$
$-7 + +4 = -3$
$-4 - 7 = -11$
$7 + +4 = 11$
$4 - 7 = -3$
$7 - 4 = 3$

Column 3

$-4 + 7 = 3$
$0 + +4 = 4$
$7 + 4 = 11$
$-7 - 4 = -11$
$0 - 4 = -4$
$4 + -4 = 0$
$0 + +4 = 4$
$-7 + +4 = -3$
$4 - 4 = 0$
$0 + -4 = -4$

Key Points from Demo Video – Lesson 2
Adding and Subtracting Integers

Lesson 2 gives students practice applying the rules that they learned in Lesson 1 for adding and subtracting positive and negative integers. Adding and subtracting zero is also included in this lesson.

The integers 3, –3, 5, –5, and 0 are added to and subtracted from each other.

Students should take their time and work carefully, paying close attention to the signs (positive and negative) and operations (addition and subtraction). The purpose of this lesson is accuracy, not just speed, so <u>do not</u> use it as a Speed Drill.

As shown in the previous lesson, students should not subtract integers. Instead, use **two strokes** to add the opposite.

If necessary, students can use the extra white space to draw positives and negatives, then use zero pairs and the sports analogy of the "positive team" and "negative team" to find the answer.

Remember, the required score for this lesson (and all lessons) is 100%, so be sure students correct any mistakes.

Key Points from Demo Video – Lesson 3-1
Shortcut for Subtracting a Positive Integer from Another Integer

In Part 1, students follow along with their instructor to learn another method for subtracting a positive integer from another integer. They are already familiar with Method 1: Don't subtract integers. Draw two strokes to add the opposite.

In Method 2, there is a shortcut for subtracting a positive integer from another integer. You do not need to draw two strokes to add the opposite. Instead, interpret the subtraction sign (–) as a negative sign, as shown in the demo video.

Compare the problem 3 – 5 = _____ in Method 1 and in Method 2. After drawing two strokes in Method 1, the problem becomes 3 + –5 = _____. There is a positive 3 and a negative 5.

In Method 2, interpret the subtraction sign (–) as a negative sign. Now, notice that the positive 3 and negative 5 have been circled. This matches the positive 3 and negative 5 that have been circled in Method 1. There's no need to draw two strokes when subtracting a positive integer from another integer.

Lesson 3-2: Shortcut for Subtracting a Positive Integer from Another Integer

Part 1: Review the two methods for subtracting a *positive* integer (shown in bold) from another integer (either positive or negative). As shown in the Lesson 3 demo video, Method 2 involves interpreting the subtraction sign (–) as a negative sign.

Method 1
Don't subtract integers. Draw
two strokes to add the opposite.

④ + ⊝9 = −5
5 + −7 = −2
6 + −2 = 4
−3 + −8 = −11
−2 + −6 = −8

Method 2
Interpret the subtraction
sign (–) as a negative sign.

④ ⊝ 9 = −5
⑥ ⊝ 2 = 4
⊝3 ⊝ 8 = −11
⑤ ⊝ 7 = −2
⊝2 ⊝ 6 = −8

Subtracting Integers

Original Rule: "Don't subtract integers." Instead, draw two strokes to add the opposite.

More Specific Rule: Don't subtract **negative** integers. Instead, draw two strokes to add the opposite.

There is a shortcut for subtracting a **positive** integer. Interpret the subtraction sign (–) as a negative sign.

Part 2: Solve. Remember to use the shortcut for subtracting a *positive* integer from another integer. Also, remember not to subtract *negative* integers. Instead, draw two strokes and add the opposite. Work carefully, and don't rush.

Column 1	Column 2	Column 3
−9 + +5 = −4	−9 + +5 = −4	5 + −5 = 0
5 + +9 = 14	−5 − 9 = −14	0 + +5 = 5
−5 + +5 = 0	9 + +5 = 14	−9 + +5 = −4
−5 + +9 = 4	5 − 9 = −4	5 − 5 = 0
9 + +5 = 14	9 − 5 = 4	0 + −5 = −5
(−5) (− 9) = −14	5 + +5 = 10	−5 + 9 = 4
(9) (− 5) = 4	5 + +9 = 14	0 + +5 = 5
(−9) (− 5) = −14	−5 + +9 = 4	9 + 5 = 14
(5) (− 9) = −4	−9 − 5 = −14	−9 + −5 = −14
(−5) (− 5) = −10	−5 + +5 = 0	0 − 5 = −5

Additional Practice – Lesson 3-2
Shortcut for Subtracting a Positive Integer from Another Integer

As shown in the previous lesson, there is a shortcut for subtracting a positive integer from another integer. You do not need to draw two strokes to add the opposite. Instead, interpret the subtraction sign (–) as a negative sign, as shown in the demo video.

KEY LESSON
⊙━ᵣ

Lesson 4-1: Multiplying and Dividing Integers Demo

Part 1: Follow along with your instructor and with the demo video to complete this lesson.

Multiplying and dividing integers is much **easier** than adding and subtracting integers.

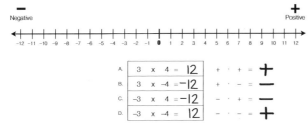

A.	3 x 4 = 12	+ · + =	**+**
B.	3 x −4 = −12	+ · − =	**−**
C.	−3 x 4 = −12	− · + =	**−**
D.	−3 x −4 = 12	− · − =	**+**

Multiplying Integers

1. Negative and negative cancel.

Dividing Integers

1. Negative and negative cancel.

Part 2: Multiply or divide.

Column 1	Column 2	Column 3
5 x 6 = 30	−6 x 5 = −30	0 ÷ −5 = 0
−5 x 6 = −30	30 ÷ −5 = −6	6 x −5 = −30
−5 x −6 = 30	6 x 0 = 0	0 x −5 = 0
5 x −6 = −30	−30 ÷ −5 = 6	−6 x 0 = 0
−30 ÷ 5 = −6	−6 x −5 = 30	30 ÷ 5 = 6

Key Points from Demo Video – Lesson 4-1
Multiplying and Dividing Integers Demo

The demo video for Lesson 4-1 shows students that multiplying and dividing integers is actually much easier than adding and subtracting integers. The single, easy-to-remember rule for multiplying and dividing integers is:

- Negative and negative cancel.

Just like in Lesson 1-1, the kangaroo will end up jumping backwards in certain situations. For example, in the problem −3 x −4, the kangaroo will jump −4 spaces "negative three times." This means it will jump −4 spaces **backwards** three times.

If you are *facing* the negative direction but you also *jump backwards*, you end up in positive territory. This is why negative and negative cancel each other out.

Name_____

Lesson 4-2: Multiplying and Dividing Integers

Part 1: Review the rules for multiplying and dividing integers.

Multiplying and dividing integers is much **easier** than adding and subtracting integers.

Multiplying Integers

1.  Negative and negative cancel.

A.	+	·	+	=	+	E.	−	·	+	=	−
B.	+	·	−	=	−	F.	−	·	−	=	+
C.	−	·	+	=	−	G.	+	·	+	=	+
D.	−	·	−	=	+	H.	+	·	−	=	−

Dividing Integers

1. 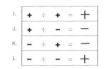 Negative and negative cancel.

I.	+	÷	+	=	+	M.	+	÷	−	=	−
J.	+	÷	−	=	−	N.	−	÷	+	=	−
K.	−	÷	+	=	−	O.	−	÷	−	=	+
L.	−	÷	−	=	+	P.	+	÷	+	=	+

Part 2: Multiply or divide.

Column 1
−4 × 3 = −12
12 ÷ −3 = −4
4 × 0 = 0
−12 ÷ −3 = 4
−4 × −3 = 12

Column 2
0 ÷ −3 = 0
4 × −3 = −12
0 × −3 = 0
−4 × 0 = 0
12 ÷ 3 = 4

Column 3
3 × 4 = 12
−3 × 4 = −12
−3 × −4 = 12
3 × −4 = −12
−12 ÷ 3 = −4

Making Sense of Integers | © MathFluency.com | **Teachers: Log in for demo videos.** 17

KEY LESSON

Name_____

Lesson 5-1: Adding, Subtracting, Multiplying, and Dividing Integers

Directions: Add, subtract, multiply, or divide. This assignment covers every possible combination, so **don't rush.** Work carefully, and focus on the signs and operations. Remember to use the shortcut for subtracting a positive integer from another integer.

Column 1
2 + −6 = −4
−2 + 6 = 4
−2 − 2 = −4
2 + 0 = 2
−2 + −6 = −8
−6 + +2 = −4
0 + +2 = 2
−2 + +2 = 0
−2 − 6 = −8
2 + +2 = 4
−4 ÷ 2 = −2
−12 ÷ −6 = 2
6 × −2 = −12
2 + +2 = 4
2 × −6 = −12
0 ÷ −2 = 0
−2 × 6 = −12
−4 ÷ −2 = 2
2 × 0 = 0
−2 × −6 = 12
6 + 2 = 8
6 − 2 = 4
0 + 2 = 2
2 − 0 = 2
−6 + −2 = −8

Column 2
12 ÷ −6 = −2
4 ÷ 2 = 2
−2 × −2 = 4
0 × −2 = 0
−2 × 0 = 0
2 + 2 = 4
2 − 6 = −4
−2 + +2 = 0
−2 − 0 = −2
2 × 2 = 4
0 − 2 = −2
−6 + 2 = −4
6 + +2 = 8
12 ÷ 2 = 6
4 ÷ −2 = −2
0 − 2 = −2
0 ÷ −2 = 0
−2 − 6 = −8
0 ÷ 2 = 0
−6 × 2 = −12
2 + −2 = 0
−12 ÷ 6 = −2
0 ÷ 2 = 0
−12 ÷ −2 = 6
2 × −2 = −4

Column 3
6 × 2 = 12
0 × 2 = 0
12 ÷ 6 = 2
0 ÷ 2 = 0
−6 × −2 = 12
−12 ÷ 2 = −6
−2 × 2 = −4
12 ÷ −2 = −6
6 + −2 = 4
−6 − 2 = −8
2 × 6 = 12
12 ÷ −6 = −2
0 + +2 = 2
0 × −2 = 0
2 + +6 = 8
−2 + 2 = 0
−2 + +6 = 4
2 + 6 = 8
−6 + +2 = −4
0 + −2 = −2
−6 + +2 = −4
2 − 2 = 0
−2 + −2 = −4
0 + −2 = −2
−2 + 0 = −2

18 Making Sense of Integers | © MathFluency.com | **Teachers: Log in for demo videos.**

Additional Practice – Lesson 4-2
Multiplying and Dividing Integers Demo

Multiplying and dividing integers is easier than adding and subtracting integers. The single, easy-to-remember rule for multiplying and dividing integers is:

• Negative and negative cancel.

Key Points from Demo Video – Lesson 5-1
Adding, Subtracting, Multiplying, and Dividing Integers

In Lesson 5-1, students practice adding, subtracting, multiplying, and dividing integers.

Students must be especially careful during this lesson because the procedure for adding and subtracting integers is different from the procedure for multiplying and dividing integers.

The integers 2, −2, 6, −6, and 0 are added to, subtracted from, and multiplied by each other.

Additionally, the integers 4, −4, 12, −12, and 0 are divided by 2, −2, 6, and −6.

Just like in Lessons 2 and 3, this is an exercise in accuracy and attention to detail, so <u>do not</u> use it as a Speed Drill.

Instead, students should pay attention to the signs (positive and negative) and operations (addition, subtraction, multiplication, and division).

Remember, the required score for this lesson (and all lessons) is 100%, so be sure students correct any mistakes.

Lesson 5-2: Adding, Subtracting, Multiplying, and Dividing Integers

Directions: Add, subtract, multiply, or divide. This assignment covers every possible combination, so **don't rush.** Work carefully, and focus on the signs and operations. Remember to use the shortcut for subtracting a positive integer from another integer.

Column 1	Column 2	Column 3
5 + −3 = 2	15 ÷ −3 = −5	3 x 5 = 15
−5 + 3 = −2	5 ÷ 5 = 1	0 x 5 = 0
−5 − 5 = −10	−5 x −5 = 25	15 ÷ 3 = 5
5 + 0 = 5	0 x −5 = 0	0 ÷ 5 = 0
−5 + −3 = −8	−5 x 0 = 0	−3 x −5 = 15
−3 + +5 = 2	5 + 5 = 10	−15 ÷ 5 = −3
0 + +5 = 5	5 − 3 = 2	−5 x 5 = −25
−5 + +5 = 0	−5 + +5 = 0	15 ÷ −5 = −3
−5 − 3 = −8	−5 − 0 = −5	3 + −5 = −2
5 + +5 = 10	5 x 5 = 25	−3 − 5 = −8
−5 ÷ 5 = −1	0 − 5 = −5	5 x 3 = 15
−15 ÷ −3 = 5	−3 + 5 = 2	15 ÷ −3 = −5
3 x −5 = −15	3 + +5 = 8	0 + +5 = 5
5 + +5 = 10	15 ÷ 5 = 3	0 x −5 = 0
5 x −3 = −15	5 ÷ −5 = −1	5 + +3 = 8
0 ÷ −5 = 0	0 − 5 = −5	−5 + 5 = 0
−5 x 3 = −15	0 ÷ −5 = 0	−5 + +3 = −2
−5 ÷ −5 = 1	−5 − 3 = −8	5 + 3 = 8
5 x 0 = 0	0 ÷ 5 = 0	−3 + +5 = 2
−5 x −3 = 15	−3 x 5 = −15	0 + −5 = −5
3 + 5 = 8	5 + −5 = 0	−3 + +5 = 2
3 − 5 = −2	−15 ÷ 3 = −5	5 − 5 = 0
0 + 5 = 5	0 ÷ 5 = 0	−5 + −5 = −10
5 − 0 = 5	−15 ÷ −5 = 3	0 + −5 = −5
−3 + −5 = −8	5 x −5 = −25	−5 + 0 = −5

Making Sense of Integers | © MathFluency.com | **Teachers: Log in for demo videos.**   19

Lesson 6-1: Adding, Subtracting, Multiplying, and Dividing Integers

Name_____

Directions: Add, subtract, multiply, or divide. This assignment covers every possible combination, so **don't rush.** Work carefully, and focus on the signs and operations. Remember to use the shortcut for subtracting a positive integer from another integer.

Column 1	Column 2	Column 3
3 + −6 = −3	18 ÷ −6 = −3	6 x 3 = 18
−3 + 6 = 3	9 ÷ 3 = 3	0 x 3 = 0
−3 − 3 = −6	−3 x −3 = 9	18 ÷ 6 = 3
3 + 0 = 3	0 x −3 = 0	0 ÷ 3 = 0
−3 + −6 = −9	−3 x 0 = 0	−6 x −3 = 18
−6 + +3 = −3	3 + 3 = 6	−18 ÷ 3 = −6
0 + +3 = 3	3 − 6 = −3	−3 x 3 = −9
−3 + +3 = 0	−3 + +3 = 0	18 ÷ −3 = −6
−3 − 6 = −9	−3 − 0 = −3	6 + −3 = 3
3 + +3 = 6	3 x 3 = 9	−6 − 3 = −9
−9 ÷ 3 = −3	0 − 3 = −3	3 x 6 = 18
−18 ÷ −6 = 3	−6 + 3 = −3	18 ÷ −6 = −3
6 x −3 = −18	6 + +3 = 9	0 + +3 = 3
3 + +3 = 6	18 ÷ 3 = 6	0 x −3 = 0
3 x −6 = −18	9 ÷ −3 = −3	3 + +6 = 9
0 ÷ −3 = 0	0 − 3 = −3	−3 + 3 = 0
−3 x 6 = −18	0 ÷ −3 = 0	−3 + +6 = 3
−9 ÷ −3 = 3	−3 − 6 = −9	3 + 6 = 9
3 x 0 = 0	0 ÷ 3 = 0	−6 + +3 = −3
−3 x −6 = 18	−6 x 3 = −18	0 + −3 = −3
6 + 3 = 9	3 + −3 = 0	−6 + +3 = −3
6 − 3 = 3	−18 ÷ 6 = −3	3 − 3 = 0
0 + 3 = 3	0 ÷ 3 = 0	−3 + −3 = −6
3 − 0 = 3	−18 ÷ −3 = 6	0 + −3 = −3
−6 + −3 = −9	3 x −3 = −9	−3 + 0 = −3

20   Making Sense of Integers | © MathFluency.com | **Teachers: Log in for demo videos.**

Additional Practice – Lesson 5-2
Adding, Subtracting, Multiplying, and Dividing Integers

In Lesson 5-2, students practice adding, subtracting, multiplying, and dividing integers.

Students must be especially careful during this lesson because the procedure for adding and subtracting integers is different from the procedure for multiplying and dividing integers.

This is an exercise in accuracy and attention to detail, so do not use it as a Speed Drill.

Instead, students should pay attention to the signs (positive and negative) and operations (addition, subtraction, multiplication, and division).

Remember, the required score for this lesson (and all lessons) is 100%, so be sure students correct any mistakes.

Key Points from Demo Video – Lesson 6-1
Adding, Subtracting, Multiplying, and Dividing Integers

In Lesson 6-1, students practice adding, subtracting, multiplying, and dividing integers.

Students must be especially careful during this lesson because the procedure for adding and subtracting integers is different from the procedure for multiplying and dividing integers.

The integers 3, −3, 6, −6, and 0 are added to, subtracted from, and multiplied by each other.

Additionally, the integers 9, −9, 18, −18, and 0 are divided by 3, −3, 6, and −6.

Just like in Lessons 5, this is an exercise in accuracy and attention to detail, so do not use it as a Speed Drill.

Instead, students should pay attention to the signs (positive and negative) and operations (addition, subtraction, multiplication, and division).

Remember, the required score for this lesson (and all lessons) is 100%, so be sure students correct any mistakes.

46   Making Sense of Integers | © MathFluency.com | **Teachers: Log in for demo videos.**

Lesson 6-2: Adding, Subtracting, Multiplying, and Dividing Integers

Directions: Add, subtract, multiply, or divide. This assignment covers every possible combination, so *don't rush.* Work carefully, and focus on the signs and operations. Remember to use the shortcut for subtracting a positive integer from another integer.

Column 1	Column 2	Column 3
8 + −7 = 1	56 ÷ −7 = −8	7 x 8 = 56
−8 + 7 = −1	64 ÷ 8 = 8	0 x 8 = 0
−8 − 8 = −16	−8 x −8 = 64	56 ÷ 7 = 8
8 + 0 = 8	0 x −8 = 0	0 ÷ 8 = 0
−8 + −7 = −15	−8 x 0 = 0	−7 x −8 = 56
−7 + +8 = 1	8 + 8 = 16	−56 ÷ 8 = −7
0 + +8 = 8	8 − 7 = 1	−8 x 8 = −64
−8 + +8 = 0	−8 + +8 = 0	56 ÷ −8 = −7
−8 − 7 = −15	−8 − 0 = −8	7 + −8 = −1
8 + +8 = 16	8 x 8 = 64	−7 − 8 = −15
−64 ÷ 8 = −8	0 − 8 = −8	8 x 7 = 56
−56 ÷ −7 = 8	−7 + 8 = 1	56 ÷ −7 = −8
7 x −8 = −56	7 + +8 = 15	0 + +8 = 8
8 + +8 = 16	56 ÷ 8 = 7	0 x −8 = 0
8 x −7 = −56	64 ÷ −8 = −8	8 + +7 = 15
0 ÷ −8 = 0	0 − 8 = −8	−8 + 8 = 0
−8 x 7 = −56	0 ÷ −8 = 0	−8 + +7 = −1
−64 ÷ −8 = 8	−8 − 7 = −15	8 + 7 = 15
8 x 0 = 0	0 ÷ 8 = 0	−7 + +8 = 1
−8 x −7 = 56	−7 x 8 = −56	0 + −8 = −8
7 + 8 = 15	8 + −8 = 0	−7 + +8 = 1
7 − 8 = −1	−56 ÷ 7 = −8	8 − 8 = 0
0 + 8 = 8	0 ÷ 8 = 0	−8 + −8 = −16
8 − 0 = 8	−56 ÷ −8 = 7	0 + −8 = −8
−7 + −8 = −15	8 x −8 = −64	−8 + 0 = −8

Additional Practice – Lesson 6-2
Adding, Subtracting, Multiplying, and Dividing Integers

In Lesson 6-2, students practice adding, subtracting, multiplying, and dividing integers.

Students must be especially careful during this lesson because the procedure for adding and subtracting integers is different from the procedure for multiplying and dividing integers.

This is an exercise in accuracy and attention to detail, so <u>do not</u> use it as a Speed Drill.

Instead, students should pay attention to the signs (positive and negative) and operations (addition, subtraction, multiplication, and division).

Remember, the required score for this lesson (and all lessons) is 100%, so be sure students correct any mistakes.

KEY LESSON

Lesson 7: Sea Level, Above Sea Level, and Below Sea Level

Directions: Using integers and feet, label the *elevation or depth* of the objects in the diagram. Then, in each problem, find how much <u>higher</u> the first object is located compared to the second object (measured in feet).

A. elevation of palm tree vs. depth of fish	B. depth of fish vs. depth of sea star	C. depth of sailboat vs. depth of sea star
8 + +4 = 12ft	−4 + +8 = 4ft	0 + +8 = 8ft
D. elevation of shovel/pail vs. depth of fish	**E.** elevation of palm tree elevation of shovel/pail	**F.** depth of beach ball vs. depth of sailboat
3 + +4 = 7ft	8 − 3 = 5ft	0 − 0 = 0ft
G. object with the highest elevation vs. object with the greatest depth	**H.** elevation of shovel/pail vs. depth of sea star	**I.** height of the sailboat from the top of the mast to the bottom of the keel
8 + +8 = 16ft	3 + +8 = 11ft	7 + +2 = 9ft

Definitions

Sea Level: the average height of the ocean's surface
Elevation: the height above sea level
Depth: the distance below sea level

Elevations and Depths

beach ball: floating at sea level (0 feet)
sailboat: floating at sea level
shovel and pail: 3 ft above sea level
palm tree: 8 ft above sea level
fish: 4 ft below sea level
sea star: sitting on the ocean floor, 8 ft below the surface

Information for Problem I Only

sailboat's mast: 7 ft above sea level
sailboat's keel: 2 ft below the surface

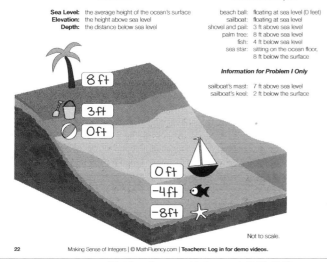

8 ft
3 ft
0 ft
0 ft
−4 ft
−8 ft

Not to scale.

Key Points from Demo Video – Lesson 7
Sea Level, Above Sea Level, and Below Sea Level

In Lesson 7, students use their skills in adding and subtracting integers to work with elevation and depth.

The diagram shows a number of objects that are at sea level, above sea level, or below sea level. Students must fill out the diagram with the given elevations or depths.

Then, for each problem, students must find out how much higher the first object is compared to the second object. Be sure students include the units (feet) in their answers.

In problem I, students must find the total height of the sailboat from the top of the mast (7 feet above sea level) to the bottom of the keel (2 feet below the surface).

Lesson 8: Increases or Decreases in Temperature

Directions: On a mountain summit, the following temperatures were recorded over a 24-hour period from midnight Monday to midnight Tuesday. Write the temperature at the times shown, and indicate whether the temperature got warmer, colder, or stayed the same from one time period to the next. Find the increase or decrease in temperature.

Example: 3 p.m. → 9 p.m. 3° → -2° colder -2 − 3 = -5°	A. 9 p.m. → 12 a.m. (Tue.) -2° → -5° colder -5 + +2 = -3°	B. 3 a.m. → 3 p.m. -5° → 3° warmer 3 + +5 = 8°
C. 12 p.m. → 3 p.m. 2° → 3° warmer 3 − 2 = 1°	D. 6 a.m. → 9 p.m. -2° → -2° same -2 + +2 = 0°	E. 3 p.m. → 6 p.m. 3° → 1° colder 1 − 3 = -2°
F. 12 p.m. → 9 p.m. 2° → -2° colder -2 − 2 = -4°	G. 3 a.m. → 9 a.m. -5° → 0° warmer 0 + +5 = 5°	H. lowest → highest temperature -7° → 3° warmer 3 + +7 = 10°

Lesson 9-1: Adding and Subtracting Multi-digit Numbers in Your Head

The next set of lessons involve adding and subtracting multi-digit integers. In order to save you time, it will help if you are able to do some of these problems in your head. Adding and subtracting multi-digit numbers in your head was covered in the book *Multi-digit Addition & Subtraction*. This lesson provides a review.

Part 1: Use **Stepping Stones** to find the difference in your head. Use the hint if necessary.

A. 23 − 14 = 9 Stepping Stone: 20 Think: 6 + 3 = 9	B. 101 − 93 = 8 Stepping Stone: 100 Think: 7 + 1 = 8	C. 165 − 93 = 72 Stepping Stone: 100 Think: 7 + 65 = 72
D. 101 − 34 = 67 Stepping Stone: 100 Think: 66 + 1 = 67	E. 93 − 34 = 59 Stepping Stones: 40 and 90 6 + 50 + 3 = 59	F. 65 − 28 = 37 Stepping Stones: 30 and 60 2 + 30 + 5 = 37

Part 2: Use the standard algorithm to find the difference in your head. These problems do not involve regrouping.

G.
  7 6
− 3 4
  4 2
	H.
	  8 9
	− 1 6
	  7 3
		I.
		  4 8 5
		− 3 1
		  4 5 4

Part 3: Find the sums in your head.

J. 800 + 40 + 2 = 842	K. 140 + 10 + 6 = 156	L. 140 + 16 = 156	M. 110 + 15 = 125

Part 4: Find the sum in your head (add the place values from **left to right**).

N. 23 + 34 = 57 Think: 50 + 7	O. 14 + 34 = 48 Think: 40 + 8	P. 93 + 14 = 107 Think: 100 + 7	Q. 165 + 23 = 188 Think: 100 + 80 + 8
R. 67 + 89 = 156 Think: 140 + 16	S. 89 + 58 = 147 Think: 130 + 17	T. 26 + 87 = 113 Think: 100 + 13	U. 78 + 47 = 125 Think: 110 + 15

Key Points from Demo Video – Lesson 8
Increases or Decreases in Temperature

The previous lesson used elevation and depth to provide students with practice adding and subtracting integers.

In Lesson 8, students use temperatures to practice adding and subtracting integers. This lesson includes the temperature of 0° as well as temperatures above 0° and below 0°.

The graph shows the temperature on a mountain summit during a 24-hour period from 12:00 a.m. Monday to 12:00 a.m. Tuesday.

The example asks students to find the temperatures at the times shown. Then, they must indicate whether the temperature got warmer, got colder, or stayed the same from one period to the next. Finally, they must find the actual change in temperature.

Most of the information in the example has been filled out. Students complete the example with their instructor to find that the change in temperature from 3:00 p.m. to 9:00 p.m. was –5°.

Students then complete the rest of the problems.

Key Points from Demo Video – Lesson 9-1
Adding and Subtracting Multi-digit Numbers in Your Head

Lesson 9-1 is a review of adding and subtracting multi-digit numbers in your head, including using **Stepping Stones.** These skills were previously covered in the books *Multi-digit Addition & Subtraction* and in *Easy Breezy Addition & Subtraction*.

Lesson 9-1 is important because if students can perform some calculations accurately in their head, it will make it easier for them to complete Lesson 10, which covers multi-digit gains and losses in elevation.

Name_____

Lesson 9-2: Adding and Subtracting Multi-digit Numbers in Your Head

The next set of lessons involve adding and subtracting multi-digit integers. In order to save you time, it will help if you are able to do some of these problems in your head. Adding and subtracting multi-digit numbers in your head was covered in the book *Multi-digit Addition & Subtraction*. This lesson provides a review.

Part 1: Use *Stepping Stones* to find the difference in your head. Use the hint if necessary.

A.	B.	C.
85 − 77 = **8**	106 − 97 = **9**	182 − 95 = **87**
Stepping Stone: 80	Stepping Stone: 100	Stepping Stone: 100
Think: **3** + **5** = **8**	Think: **3** + **6** = **9**	Think: **5** + **82** = **87**
D.	E.	F.
106 − 48 = **58**	73 − 47 = **26**	84 − 67 = **17**
Stepping Stone: 100	Stepping Stones: 50 and 70	Stepping Stones: 70 and 80
Think: **52** + **6** = **58**	**3** + **20** + **3** = **26**	**3** + **10** + **4** = **17**

Part 2: Use the standard algorithm to find the difference in your head. These problems do not involve regrouping.

G.	H.	I.
8 9 − 4 5 **4 4**	7 8 − 3 2 **4 6**	7 7 6 − 4 2 **7 3 4**

Part 3: Find the sums in your head.

J.	K.	L.	M.
270 + 10 + 3 = **283**	270 + 13 = **283**	130 + 19 = **149**	450 + 17 = **467**

Part 4: Find the sum in your head (add the place values from *left to right*).

N.	O.	P.	Q.
35 + 43 = **78**	56 + 42 = **98**	84 + 24 = **108**	453 + 46 = **499**
Think: **70** + **8**	Think: **90** + **8**	Think: **100** + **8**	Think: **400** + **90** + **9**
R.	S.	T.	U.
74 + 98 = **172**	37 + 46 = **83**	65 + 48 = **113**	89 + 84 = **173**
Think: **160** + **12**	Think: **70** + **13**	Think: **100** + **13**	Think: **160** + **13**

Additional Practice – Lesson 9-2
Adding and Subtracting Multi-digit Numbers in Your Head

Lesson 9-2 is a review of adding and subtracting multi-digit numbers in your head, including using **Stepping Stones.** These skills were previously covered in the books *Multi-digit Addition & Subtraction* and in *Easy Breezy Addition & Subtraction.*

Lesson 9-2 is important because if students can perform some calculations accurately in their head, it will make it easier for them to complete Lesson 10, which covers multi-digit gains and losses in elevation.

Name_____

Lesson 10: Elevation Gain or Loss

Directions: Write the elevation at each point. Indicate whether the elevation got higher or lower from one point to the next. Find the elevation gain or loss.

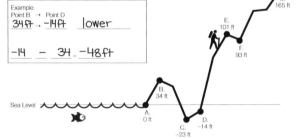

Example:
Point B → Point D
34 ft → −14 ft   lower

−14 − 34 = −48 ft

1.	2.
Point A → Point B	Point B → Point C
0 ft → 34 ft higher	34 ft → −23 ft lower
34 − 0 = 34 ft	−23 − 34 = −57 ft
3.	4.
Point C → Point D	Point D → Point E
−23 ft → −14 ft higher	−14 ft → 101 ft higher
−14 + +23 = 9 ft	101 + +14 = 115 ft
5.	6.
Point E → Point F	Point F → Point G
101 ft → 93 ft lower	93 ft → 165 ft higher
93 − 101 = −8 ft	165 − 93 = 72 ft
7.	8.
Point D → Point F	lowest → highest point
−14 ft → 93 ft higher	−23 ft → 165 ft higher
93 + +14 = 107 ft	165 + +23 = 188 ft

Key Points from Demo Video – Lesson 10
Elevation Gain or Loss

In Lesson 10, students work with gains or losses in elevation.

Lesson 9 prepared students for this lesson by reviewing how to add and subtract multi-digit numbers in your head.

Students should still perform their calculations with paper and pencil if necessary, but they may be able to save some time if they can do some of these calculations accurately in their head.

The example asks students to find the elevations at the points shown. Then, they must indicate whether the elevation got higher or lower from one point to the next. Finally, they must find the actual change in elevation.

Most of the information in the example has been filled out. Students complete the rest of the example with their instructor to find that the change in elevation from Point B to Point D was −48 ft.

Lesson 11-1: Adding and Subtracting Multi-digit Integers

Directions: Solve. Only the signs and operations change from problem to problem in each set. Use the workspace to perform your calculations.

Set 1

			Workspace
A.	47 + 84 = 131	E.	47 + −84 = −37
B.	47 − 84 = −37	F.	47 + +84 = 131
C.	−47 + 84 = 37	G.	−47 + −84 = −131
D.	−47 − 84 = −131	H.	−47 + +84 = 37

Workspace:
```
  1
  84        7
+47        8̸4̸
1 31       -47
            37
```

Set 2

		Workspace
I.	573 + 3,238 = 3,811
J.	573 − 3,238 = −2,665
K.	−573 + 3,238 = 2,665
L.	−573 − 3,238 = −3,811
M.	573 + −3,238 = −2,665
N.	573 + +3,238 = 3,811
O.	−573 + −3,238 = −3,811
P.	−573 + +3,238 = 2,665

Workspace:
```
  1 1          2 11
3,2 3 8       3̸,2̸3 8
+  5 7 3      -  5 7 3
3,8 1 1        2,6 6 5
```

Set 3

		Workspace
Q.	−5,347 + +4,759 = −588
R.	−5,347 − 4,759 = −10,106
S.	5,347 + +4,759 = 10,106
T.	5,347 − 4,759 = 588
U.	−5,347 + −4,759 = −10,106
V.	5,347 + −4,759 = 588
W.	5,347 + 4,759 = 10,106
X.	−5,347 + 4,759 = −588

Workspace:
```
  1 1 1          4 12 13
5 3 4 7         5̸ 3̸ 4̸ 7̸
+4 7 5 9        -4 7 5 9
1 0,1 0 6          5 8 8
```

Key Points from Demo Video – Lesson 11-1
Adding and Subtracting Multi-digit Integers

In this lesson, students add and subtract two-digit, three-digit, and four-digit integers.

In each set, only the signs (positive and negative) and operations (addition and subtraction) change from problem to problem. For example, in Set 1, the integers 47, −47, 84, and −84 and added to and subtracted from each other.

Students should use the workspace to the right of each problem to perform their calculations.

Lesson 11-2: Adding and Subtracting Multi-digit Integers

Directions: Solve. Only the signs and operations change from problem to problem in each set. Use the workspace to perform your calculations.

Set 1

			Workspace
A.	58 + −93 = −35	E.	58 + 93 = 151
B.	58 + +93 = 151	F.	58 − 93 = −35
C.	−58 + −93 = −151	G.	−58 + 93 = 35
D.	−58 + +93 = 35	H.	−58 − 93 = −151

Workspace:
```
  8
9̸3          1
-5 8        9 3
  3 5      +5 8
          1 5 1
```

Set 2

		Workspace
I.	787 − 4,465 = −3,678
J.	−787 + 4,465 = 3,678
K.	−787 − 4,465 = −5,252
L.	787 + −4,465 = −3,678
M.	787 + +4,465 = 5,252
N.	−787 + −4,465 = −5,252
O.	−787 + +4,465 = 3,678
P.	787 + 4,465 = 5,252

Workspace:
```
3 13 5
4̸,4̸6̸ 5        1 1 1
-  7 8 7      4,4 6 5
3,6 7 8       +  7 8 7
               5,2 5 2
```

Set 3

		Workspace
Q.	−7,242 − 3,758 = −11,000
R.	7,242 + +3,758 = 11,000
S.	7,242 − 3,758 = 3,484
T.	−7,242 + −3,758 = −11,000
U.	7,242 + −3,758 = 3,484
V.	7,242 + 3,758 = 11,000
W.	−7,242 + 3,758 = −3,484
X.	−7,242 + +3,758 = −3,484

Workspace:
```
  1 1 1         6 11 13
7,2 4 2        7̸,2̸ 4̸ 2̸
+3,7 5 8       -3,7 5 8
1 1,0 0 0        3,4 8 4
```

Additional Practice – Lesson 11-2
Adding and Subtracting Multi-digit Integers

In this lesson, students add and subtract two-digit, three-digit, and four-digit integers.

In each set, only the signs (positive and negative) and operations (addition and subtraction) change from problem to problem. For example, in Set 1, the integers 58, −58, 93, and −93 and added to and subtracted from each other.

Students should use the workspace to the right of each problem to perform their calculations.

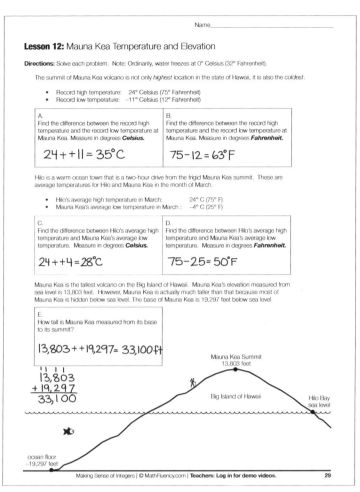

Name_____

Lesson 12: Mauna Kea Temperature and Elevation

Directions: Solve each problem. Note: Ordinarily, water freezes at 0° Celsius (32° Fahrenheit).

The summit of Mauna Kea volcano is not only *highest* location in the state of Hawaii, it is also the *coldest.*

- Record high temperature: 24° Celsius (75° Fahrenheit)
- Record low temperature: –11° Celsius (12° Fahrenheit)

A.
Find the difference between the record high temperature and the record low temperature at Mauna Kea. Measure in degrees **Celsius.**

$24 + +11 = 35°C$

B.
Find the difference between the record high temperature and the record low temperature at Mauna Kea. Measure in degrees **Fahrenheit.**

$75 - 12 = 63°F$

Hilo is a warm ocean town that is a two-hour drive from the frigid Mauna Kea summit. These are average temperatures for Hilo and Mauna Kea in the month of March.

- Hilo's average high temperature in March: 24° C (75° F)
- Mauna Kea's average low temperature in March :   –4° C (25° F)

C.
Find the difference between Hilo's average high temperature and Mauna Kea's average low temperature. Measure in degrees **Celsius.**

$24 + +4 = 28°C$

D.
Find the difference between Hilo's average high temperature and Mauna Kea's average low temperature. Measure in degrees **Fahrenheit.**

$75 - 25 = 50°F$

Mauna Kea is the tallest volcano on the Big Island of Hawaii. Mauna Kea's elevation measured from sea level is 13,803 feet. However, Mauna Kea is actually much taller than that because most of Mauna Kea is hidden below sea level. The base of Mauna Kea is 19,297 feet below sea level.

E.
How tall is Mauna Kea measured from its base to its summit?

$13,803 + +19,297 = 33,100 ft$

$$\begin{array}{r} 13,803 \\ + 19,297 \\ \hline 33,100 \end{array}$$

Mauna Kea Summit
13,803 feet

Big Island of Hawaii

Hilo Bay
sea level

ocean floor
–19,297 feet

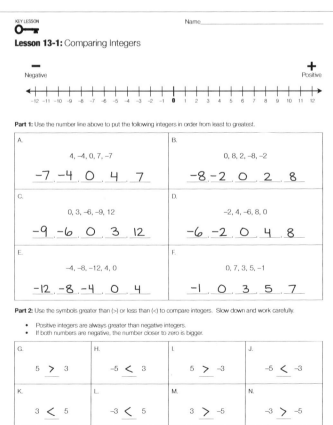

KEY LESSON

Name_____

Lesson 13-1: Comparing Integers

— Negative   **+** Positive

← | | | | | | | | | | | | **0** | | | | | | | | | | | | →
-12 -11 -10 -9 -8 -7 -6 -5 -4 -3 -2 -1   1 2 3 4 5 6 7 8 9 10 11 12

Part 1: Use the number line above to put the following integers in order from least to greatest.

A.	B.
4, –4, 0, 7, –7	0, 8, 2, –8, –2
$-7, -4, 0, 4, 7$	$-8, -2, 0, 2, 8$

C.	D.
0, 3, –6, –9, 12	–2, 4, –6, 8, 0
$-9, -6, 0, 3, 12$	$-6, -2, 0, 4, 8$

E.	F.
–4, –8, –12, 4, 0	0, 7, 3, 5, –1
$-12, -8, -4, 0, 4$	$-1, 0, 3, 5, 7$

Part 2: Use the symbols greater than (>) or less than (<) to compare integers. Slow down and work carefully.

- Positive integers are always greater than negative integers.
- If both numbers are negative, the number closer to zero is bigger.

G.	H.	I.	J.
5 $>$ 3	–5 $<$ 3	5 $>$ –3	–5 $<$ –3

K.	L.	M.	N.
3 $<$ 5	–3 $<$ 5	3 $>$ –5	–3 $>$ –5

O.	P.	Q.	R.
5 $>$ 0	–5 $<$ 0	0 $<$ 5	0 $>$ –5

Key Points from Demo Video – Lesson 12
Mauna Kea Temperature and Elevation

In Lesson 12, students solve temperature and elevation problems involving the summit of Mauna Kea volcano, which is the *highest* and *coldest* location in the state of Hawaii.

Students will work with temperatures above and below zero degrees Celsius. They will also work with temperatures measured in degrees Fahrenheit.

In problem E, students are asked to find the total height of Mauna Kea. Mauna Kea's elevation measured from sea level is 13,803 feet. However, Mauna Kea is actually much taller than that because most of Mauna Kea is hidden below sea level. The base of Mauna Kea is 19,297 feet below sea level.

When Mauna Kea is measured from its base 19,297 feet below sea level to its summit 13,803 feet above sea level, its total height is 33,100 feet.

This makes Mauna Kea taller than Mt. Everest (29,029 feet). While Mt. Everest is the *highest* mountain in the world (measured from sea level), Mauna Kea is the *tallest* mountain in the world (measured from its base to its summit).

Key Points from Demo Video – Lesson 13-1
Comparing Integers

In Lesson 13-1, students compare the magnitude of integers.

In Part 1, students must put five integers in order from least to greatest. Box A, for example, uses the integers 4, –4, 0, 7, and –7. When students put them in order from least to greatest, they will end up with:

- –7, –4, 0, 4, 7

Students should use the number line to help them since it will give them a sense of where the positive and negative integers lie in relation to 0 on the number line.

In Part 2, students use the greater than (>) or less than (<) symbols to compare integers. Students should slow down and work carefully. Keep the following in mind:

- Positive integers are always greater than negative integers.
- If both numbers are negative, then the number closer to zero is bigger.

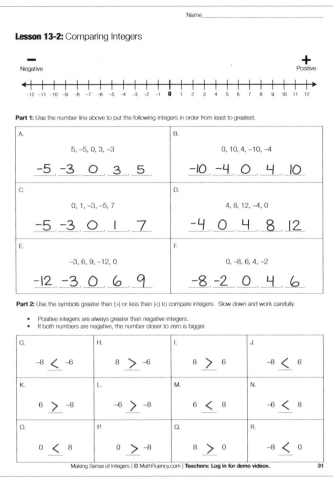

Lesson 13-2: Comparing Integers

Name_____

Negative −   Positive +

−12 −11 −10 −9 −8 −7 −6 −5 −4 −3 −2 −1 **0** 1 2 3 4 5 6 7 8 9 10 11 12

Part 1: Use the number line above to put the following integers in order from least to greatest.

A.	B.
5, −5, 0, 3, −3	0, 10, 4, −10, −4
−5 −3 0 3 5	−10 −4 0 4 10
C.	D.
0, 1, −3, −5, 7	4, 8, 12, −4, 0
−5 −3 0 1 7	−4 0 4 8 12
E.	F.
−3, 6, 9, −12, 0	0, −8, 6, 4, −2
−12 −3 0 6 9	−8 −2 0 4 6

Part 2: Use the symbols greater than (>) or less than (<) to compare integers. Slow down and work carefully.

- Positive integers are always greater than negative integers.
- If both numbers are negative, the number closer to zero is bigger.

G.	H.	I.	J.
−8 < −6	8 > −6	8 > 6	−8 < 6
K.	L.	M.	N.
6 > −8	−6 > −8	6 < 8	−6 < 8
O.	P.	Q.	R.
0 < 8	0 > −8	8 > 0	−8 < 0

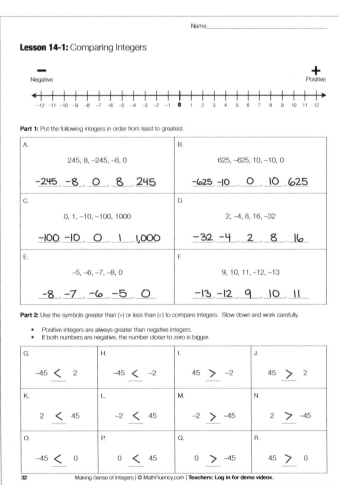

Lesson 14-1: Comparing Integers

Name_____

Negative −   Positive +

−12 −11 −10 −9 −8 −7 −6 −5 −4 −3 −2 −1 **0** 1 2 3 4 5 6 7 8 9 10 11 12

Part 1: Put the following integers in order from least to greatest.

A.	B.
245, 8, −245, −8, 0	625, −625, 10, −10, 0
−245 −8 0 8 245	−625 −10 0 10 625
C.	D.
0, 1, −10, −100, 1000	2, −4, 8, 16, −32
−100 −10 0 1 1,000	−32 −4 2 8 16
E.	F.
−5, −6, −7, −8, 0	9, 10, 11, −12, −13
−8 −7 −6 −5 0	−13 −12 9 10 11

Part 2: Use the symbols greater than (>) or less than (<) to compare integers. Slow down and work carefully.

- Positive integers are always greater than negative integers.
- If both numbers are negative, the number closer to zero is bigger.

G.	H.	I.	J.
−45 < 2	−45 < −2	45 > −2	45 > 2
K.	L.	M.	N.
2 < 45	−2 < 45	−2 > −45	2 > −45
O.	P.	Q.	R.
−45 < 0	0 < 45	0 > −45	45 > 0

Additional Practice – Lesson 13-2
Comparing Integers

In Lesson 13-2, students compare the magnitude of integers.

In Part 1, students must put five integers in order from least to greatest. Box A, for example, uses the integers 5, −5, 0, 3, and −3. When students put them in order from least to greatest, they will end up with:

- −5, −3, 0, 3, 5

Students should use the number line to help them since it will give them a sense of where the positive and negative integers lie in relation to 0 on the number line.

In Part 2, students use the greater than (>) or less than (<) symbols to compare integers. Students should slow down and work carefully. Keep the following in mind:

- Positive integers are always greater than negative integers.
- If both numbers are negative, then the number closer to zero is bigger.

Key Points from Demo Video – Lesson 14-1
Comparing Integers

In Lesson 14-1, students compare the magnitude of integers.

In Part 1, students must put five integers in order from least to greatest. Box A, for example, uses the integers 245, 8, −245, −8, and 0. When students put them in order from least to greatest, they will end up with:

- −245, −8, 0, 8, 245

Students should use the number line to help them since it will give them a sense of where the positive and negative integers lie in relation to 0 on the number line.

In Part 2, students use the greater than (>) or less than (<) symbols to compare integers. Students should slow down and work carefully. Keep the following in mind:

- Positive integers are always greater than negative integers.
- If both numbers are negative, then the number closer to zero is bigger.

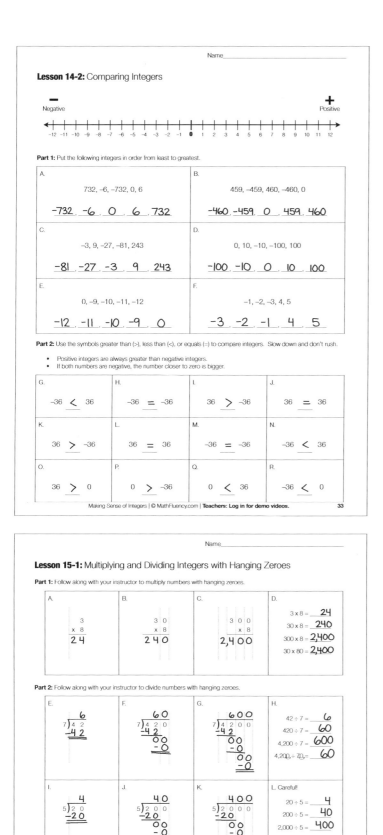

Comparing Integers

In Lesson 14-2, students compare the magnitude of integers.

In Part 1, students must put five integers in order from least to greatest. Box A, for example, uses the integers 732, –6, –732, 0, and 6. When students put them in order from least to greatest, they will end up with:

- –732, –6, 0, 6, 732

Students should use the number line to help them since it will give them a sense of where the positive and negative integers lie in relation to 0 on the number line.

In Part 2, students use the greater than symbol (>), less than symbol (<), or equals sign (=) to compare integers. Students should slow down and work carefully. Keep the following in mind:

- Positive integers are always greater than negative integers.
- If both numbers are negative, then the number closer to zero is bigger.

Key Points from Demo Video – Lesson 15-1

Multiplying and Dividing Integers with Hanging Zeroes

In Part 1, students review the shortcut for multiplying with hanging zeroes. This skill was previously covered in the book *Making Sense of Conversions*.

In Part 2, students learn the shortcut for dividing numbers with hanging zeroes.

- Problems E, F, G, and H go together.
- Problems I, J, K, and L go together.

The last problem in Box H is 4,200 ÷ 70. As was shown in the book *Making Sense of Division,* the decimal point in both 4,200 and in 70 can be moved to the left one place. This gives you 420 ÷ 7, which gives you 60.

Students should be especially careful with problem L. Students should use an index card to keep track of the hanging zeroes. In the problem 2,000 ÷ 5, students use an index card to cover up all the digits in 2,000. Sliding once to the right reveals "2," which is not divisible by 5. Sliding once more to the right reveals "20." 20 ÷ 5 gives you 4, and the two remaining hanging zeroes that were covered up with the index card give you 400.

Worksheet (Page 35)

Name_____

Lesson 15-2: Multiplying and Dividing Integers with Hanging Zeroes

Part 1: Follow along with your instructor to multiply numbers with hanging zeroes.

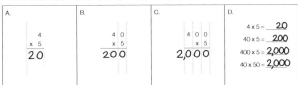

A.	B.	C.	D.
4 x 5 **20**	4 0 x 5 **200**	4 0 0 x 5 **2,000**	4 x 5 = __20__ 40 x 5 = __200__ 400 x 5 = __2,000__ 40 x 50 = __2,000__

Part 2: Follow along with your instructor to divide numbers with hanging zeroes.

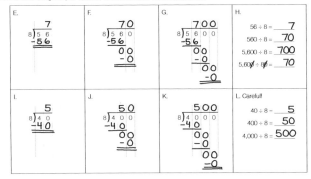

E.	F.	G.	H.
7 8)5 6 -5 6	**70** 8)5 6 0 -5 6 0 0 - 0	**700** 8)5 6 0 0 -5 6 0 0 - 0 0 0 - 0	56 ÷ 8 = __7__ 560 ÷ 8 = __70__ 5,600 ÷ 8 = __700__ 5,600 ÷ 80 = __70__
I.	J.	K.	L. Careful!
5 8)4 0 -4 0	**50** 8)4 0 0 -4 0 0 0 - 0	**500** 8)4 0 0 0 -4 0 0 0 - 0 0 0 - 0	40 ÷ 8 = __5__ 400 ÷ 8 = __50__ 4,000 ÷ 8 = __500__

Part 3: Multiply or divide.

Column 1		Column 2		Column 3	
0 ÷ -6 = **0**		6 x 7 = **42**		-7 x 60 = **-420**	
70 x -6 = **-420**		-600 x 7 = **-4,200**		4,200 ÷ -6 = **-700**	
0 x -60 = **0**		-6 x -70 = **420**		70 x 0 = **0**	
-70 x 0 = **0**		60 x -70 = **-4,200**		-42 ÷ -6 = **7**	
420 ÷ 6 = **70**		-420 ÷ 6 = **-70**		-70 x -60 = **4,200**	

Making Sense of Integers | © MathFluency.com | **Teachers: Log in for demo videos.**   35

Worksheet (Page 36)

Name_____

Lesson 16-1: Adding, Subtracting, and Multiplying Integers

Part 1: Follow along with your instructor to complete this lesson. Look for Tens, Doubles, and sums or differences that cancel each other out. Remember to use the shortcut for subtracting a positive integer from another integer.

Column 1	Column 2
2 + 4 + 6 = **12**	2 - 4 + 6 = **-8**
2 + 4 - 6 = **0**	2 - 4 + 6 = **4**
2 - 4 + 6 = **4**	-2 + 4 + 6 = **0**
2 - 4 - 6 = **-8**	-2 + 4 - 6 = **-12**
-2 + 4 + 6 = **8**	-2 + 4 + 6 = **8**
2 + 4 - 6 = **-4**	2 + 4 - 6 = **-4**
2 - 4 + 6 = **0**	2 + 4 + 6 = **-4**
-2 - 4 - 6 = **-12**	-2 + 4 + 6 = **8**
2 + -4 + 6 = **4**	-2 - 4 + 6 = **-12**
2 + 4 - 6 = **-8**	2 - 4 + 6 = **0**
2 + 4 + 6 = **12**	-2 + 4 + 6 = **-12**
2 + 4 - 6 = **0**	2 + 4 + 6 = **0**
2 + 4 + -6 = **0**	2 + 4 + 6 = **-4**
2 + 4 + 6 = **12**	-2 + 4 + 6 = **8**
-2 - 4 - 6 = **-12**	-2 + 4 + 6 = **8**

Part 2: Multiply. Remember that when multiplying integers, two negatives will cancel each other out and give you a positive.

Column 1	Column 2
2 x 4 x 6 = **48**	-2 x -4 x 6 = **48**
-2 x 4 x 6 = **-48**	2 x -4 x -6 = **48**
-2 x 4 x -6 = **48**	2 x -4 x 6 = **-48**
2 x 4 x -6 = **-48**	-2 x -4 x -6 = **-48**
-2 x -4 x -6 = **-48**	2 x -4 x -6 = **48**

36   Making Sense of Integers | © MathFluency.com | **Teachers: Log in for demo videos.**

Additional Practice – Lesson 15-2
Multiplying and Dividing Integers with Hanging Zeroes

In Part 1, students review the shortcut for multiplying with hanging zeroes. This skill was previously covered in the book *Making Sense of Conversions.*

In Part 2, students learn the shortcut for dividing numbers with hanging zeroes.

- Problems E, F, G, and H go together.
- Problems I, J, K, and L go together.

The last problem in Box H is 5,600 ÷ 80. As was shown in the book *Making Sense of Division,* the decimal point in both 5,600 and in 80 can be moved to the left one place. This gives you 560 ÷ 8, which gives you 70.

Students should be especially careful with problem L. Students should use an index card to keep track of the hanging zeroes. In the problem 4,000 ÷ 8, students use an index card to cover up all the digits in 4,000. Sliding once to the right reveals "4," which is not divisible by 8. Sliding once more to the right reveals "40." 40 ÷ 8 gives you 5, and the two remaining hanging zeroes that were covered up with the index card give you 500.

Key Points from Demo Video – Lesson 16-1
Adding, Subtracting, and Multiplying Integers

In Lesson 16-1, students follow along with their instructor to add, subtract, and multiply three integers.

Part 1 involves adding and subtracting, and it uses only the integers 2, –2, 4, –4, 6, and –6. Students should look for Tens, Doubles, and sums or differences that cancel each other out, as shown in the demo video. Also, remember to use the shortcut for subtracting a positive integer from another integer.

In Part 2, students multiply three integers with each other. Remember that when multiplying integers, two negatives will cancel each other out and give you a positive.

Again, this is an exercise in accuracy and attention to detail, so <u>do not</u> use it as a Speed Drill. Instead, students should pay attention to the signs (positive and negative) and operations (addition, subtraction, and multiplication).

Remember, the required score for this lesson (and all lessons) is 100%, so be sure students correct any mistakes.

54   *Making Sense of Integers* | © MathFluency.com | **Teachers: Log in for demo videos.**

Lesson 16-2: Adding, Subtracting, and Multiplying Integers

Name_____

Part 1: Follow along with your instructor to complete this lesson. Look for Hundreds, Doubles, and sums or differences that cancel each other out. Remember to use the shortcut for subtracting a positive integer from another integer.

Column 1

$25 + 50 + 75 = 150$
$25 + 50 - 75 = 0$
$25 + 50 + -75 = 0$
$25 + 50 + 75 = 150$
$25 - 50 - 75 = -150$
$25 + 50 + 75 = 150$
$25 + 50 - 75 = 0$
$25 - 50 + 75 = 50$
$25 - 50 - 75 = -100$
$25 + 50 + 75 = 100$
$25 + 50 - 75 = -50$
$25 - 50 + 75 = 0$
$25 - 50 - 75 = -150$
$25 + -50 + 75 = 50$
$25 + 50 - 75 = -100$

Column 2

$25 + -50 + -75 = -150$
$25 + -50 + 75 = 0$
$-25 + 50 + -75 = -50$
$25 + 50 + 75 = 100$
$-25 + 50 + 75 = 100$
$25 - 50 + -75 = -100$
$25 - 50 + 75 = 50$
$-25 + -50 + 75 = 0$
$25 + -50 - 75 = -150$
$25 + 50 + 75 = 100$
$25 + 50 - 75 = -50$
$25 + 50 + 75 = -50$
$25 + 50 + 75 = 100$
$25 - 50 + 75 = -150$
$25 - 50 + 75 = 0$

Part 2: Multiply. Remember that when multiplying integers, two negatives will cancel each other out and give you a positive.

Column 1

$1 \cdot 2 \cdot 3 \cdot 4 = 24$
$1 \cdot -2 \cdot -3 \cdot 4 = 24$
$1 \cdot 2 \cdot 3 \cdot -4 = -24$
$-1 \cdot 2 \cdot -3 \cdot 4 = -24$
$-1 \cdot -2 \cdot -3 \cdot -4 = 24$

Column 2

$-1 \cdot 2 \cdot -3 \cdot 4 = 24$
$-1 \cdot -2 \cdot -3 \cdot -4 = 24$
$1 \cdot -2 \cdot -3 \cdot -4 = -24$
$1 \cdot -2 \cdot 3 \cdot 4 = -24$
$0 \cdot -1 \cdot -2 \cdot -3 = 0$

Name_____

Lesson 17: Integer Word Problems Involving Multiplication and Division

Directions: In the first two problems in each row, write the integer and the units represented by each problem. Then, solve the last problem in each row by multiplying or dividing. **Remember to include the units in both your calculations and in the final answer.**

Example A1. Three gallons of water are emptied from a tank.	Example A2. Three gallons of water are added to a tank.	Example A3. Three gallons of water are emptied from a tank every day. Show the gain or loss in water after five days.
−3 gallons	3 gallons	$\dfrac{-3\,gal}{day} \cdot 5\,days = -15\,gal$
Example B1. A store has revenues of $420.	Example B2. A store has an expense of $420.	Example B3. A store pays off a $420 expense over a six-month period with equal payments. Show the increase or decrease in cash per month.
420 dollars	−420 dollars	$\dfrac{-\$420}{6\,mo} = \dfrac{-\$70}{mo}$
C1. $7 is deposited into a bank account.	C2. $7 is deducted from a bank account.	C3. $7 is deposited into a bank account every month. Show the increase or decrease in the account balance after twelve months.
7 dollars	−7 dollars	$\dfrac{\$7}{mo} \cdot 12\,mo = \$84$
D1. A man loses two pounds.	D2. A man gains two pounds.	D3. A man loses two pounds each week. Show the increase or decrease in weight after six weeks.
−2 lbs.	2 lbs.	$\dfrac{-2\,lbs}{wk} \cdot 6\,wk = -12\,lbs$
E1. A quarterback in a football game gains 15 yards.	E2. A quarterback loses 15 yards.	E3. A quarterback loses 15 yards in three plays. Show the average loss per play.
15 yards	−15 yards	$\dfrac{-15\,yd}{3\,plays} = \dfrac{-5\,yd}{play}$

Additional Practice – Lesson 16-2
Adding, Subtracting, and Multiplying Integers

In Lesson 16-2, students follow along with their instructor to add, subtract, and multiply three integers.

Part 1 involves adding and subtracting, and it uses only the integers 25, –25, 50, –50, 75, and –75. Students should look for Hundreds, Doubles, and sums or differences that cancel each other out. Also, remember to use the shortcut for subtracting a positive integer from another integer.

In Part 2, students multiply four integers with each other. Remember that when multiplying integers, two negatives will cancel each other out and give you a positive.

Again, this is an exercise in accuracy and attention to detail, so do not use it as a Speed Drill. Instead, students should pay attention to the signs (positive and negative) and operations (addition, subtraction, and multiplication).

Remember, the required score for this lesson (and all lessons) is 100%, so be sure students correct any mistakes.

Key Points from Demo Video – Lesson 17
Integer Word Problems Involving Multiplication and Division

In Lesson 17, each row has three problems that belong together. The first row of problems illustrates how this works.

- The **first two problems** in each row use opposite values.
  - In Example A1, a loss of three gallons is written as –3 gallons.
  - In Example A2, an addition of three gallons is written as 3 gallons.
- The **last problem** in each row uses one of the previous two values in its calculations.
  - Example A3 shows that –3 gallons per day multiplied by 5 days is –15 gallons.

The second row (Examples B1, B2, and B3) uses division instead of multiplication.

Be sure students include the units in their answers. The answer for Example B3 is –$70 per month, not just –70.

This lesson involves proportion problems and rate problems. These skills were covered previously in the book *Making Sense of Proportions*.

Lesson 18: Integer Word Problems Involving Multiplication and Division

Directions: In the first two problems in each row, write the integer and the units represented by each problem. Then, solve the last problem in each row by multiplying or dividing. *Remember to include the units in both your calculations and in the final answer.*

A1. A house increases in value by $16,000.	A2. A house decreases in value by $16,000.	A3. A house increases in value by $16,000 over four years. Show the average gain or loss per year.
16,000 dollars	−16,000 dollars	$\dfrac{\$16{,}000}{4\ \text{yr}} = \dfrac{\$4{,}000}{\text{yr}}$
B1. A running back in a football game loses 6 yards.	B2. A running back gains 6 yards.	B3. A running back gains 6 yards per carry. Show the gain after three carries.
−6 yards	6 yards	$\dfrac{6\ \text{yd}}{\text{carry}} \cdot 3\ \text{carries} = 18\ \text{yd}$
C1. $54 is deducted from a bank account.	C2. $54 is deposited into a bank account.	C3. $54 is deducted from an account over the course of six months. Show the increase or decrease in the account balance per month.
−54 dollars	54 dollars	$\dfrac{-\$54}{6\ \text{mo}} = \dfrac{-\$9}{\text{mo}}$
D1. A weightlifter gains 12 pounds.	D2. A weightlifter loses 12 pounds.	D3. A weightlifter wants to gain 12 lbs. of muscle in four months. Show the needed increase or decrease in weight per month.
12 pounds	−12 pounds	$\dfrac{12\ \text{lbs}}{4\ \text{mo}} = \dfrac{3\ \text{lbs}}{\text{mo}}$
E1. A store has revenues of $800 in cash.	E2. A store has an expense of $800.	E3. A store has revenues of $800 in cash per day. Show the increase or decrease in cash after seven days.
800 dollars	−800 dollars	$\dfrac{\$800}{\text{day}} \cdot 7\ \text{days} = \$5{,}600$

Key Points from Demo Video – Lesson 18
Integer Word Problems Involving Multiplication and Division

Lesson 18 is a continuation of Lesson 17 in which students solved integer word problems involving multiplication and division. As in the previous lesson, each row has three problems that belong together.

- The first two problems in each row use opposite values (such as 16,000 dollars and −16,000 dollars).
- The last problem in each row uses one of the previous two values in its calculations.

Be sure students include the units in their answers. The answer for Problem A3 is $4,000 per year, not just 4,000.

This lesson involves proportion problems and rate problems. These skills were covered previously in the book *Making Sense of Proportions*.

84206906R00033